Juvenile Problems and Law

LAW IN ACTION SERIES
Second Edition

RIEKES–ACKERLY
LESSONS IN LAW FOR
YOUNG PEOPLE

WEST PUBLISHING COMPANY
St. Paul   New York   Los Angeles   San Francisco

International Standard Book Number: 0–8299–1025–5
Library of Congress Catalog Card Number: 80–11394

5th Reprint—1986

FOREWORD

One way to think about the meaning of law is to consider it as a body of rules which include penalties if we violate them. This is the most direct effect law has upon us. But we must at the same time think about the effect law has for most of us who do not violate the rules; for law is the basis of a modern regulated social order under which we live. It may be viewed as a contract we all make with each other for our common good. In effect it says that you may do what you wish so long as your acts do not take away from me my same right to do what I wish. Your right to have an automobile can be exercised, unless by doing so you curb my right to own an automobile. Thus, the law makes it wrong for you to take (steal) my automobile because in doing so you infringe upon my right to own that car. This application of law to ownership of property extends in a similar way to the social and political interests of all individuals. In a democratic society it also protects you and me from arbitrary (unlawful) actions by our government against us.

The underlying principles for these rules (laws) are set forth in other laws which make up the constitution of our government. The constitution is called the organic law of a government and cannot be changed without the approval of a majority of the people or their representatives. Within the guidelines imposed by the constitution, the lawmakers (legislatures) may make detailed rules (laws) from time to time which govern our conduct.

Given these basic assumptions, what can be more reasonable than to know what these rules (laws) which govern our conduct are. This is the purpose of JUVENILE PROBLEMS AND LAW, and it is of particular importance since the laws which affect the conduct of juveniles are different from those which apply to the conduct of persons who are older than juveniles.

Ordinarily I could say that the rules for adults are different from those for juveniles, but adulthood is too vague a term to use. In what we may consider "ancient" times, there developed in England over centuries a body of law which is known as the "common law". This "common law" (which is still developing by decisions in cases heard by the courts) became the basis of our law in the United States. It is still applied by the courts, unless the legislatures specifically change it. For our present purposes we may say that under the "common law" people were divided into three groups based solely on age. First were infants. The law provided that infants could not be charged with a crime because they were incapable of having the evil intent necessary to commit a crime. The state of infancy existed from birth to seven years of age. The second group consisted of those age seven to age fourteen. Like the first group, those in the second group were presumed to be incapable of having the evil intent legally necessary to commit a crime, but this presumption could be rebutted. In other words, if the prosecution could prove that persons in this group were capable of having the evil intent, that is were mature enough to have such intent, then they could be charged with crimes and tried as adults. The third group contained all persons over fourteen years of age. Persons in this group were tried in the criminal courts as adults. Accordingly, under the old rules that applied to crimes, fourteen was the age of adulthood.

Under the old common law the age of majority or full adulthood was twenty-one. But this could be, and was in many instances, changed by state lawmakers (legislatures). The right to vote was limited to persons twenty-one years of age, but recently most states changed the age required to vote to eighteen. The right to enter into contracts, hold public office, buy liquor, work in various occupations, drive a car, marry, buy certain reading material, receive medical attention, and to retain earnings without parental consent varies depending upon the age established by laws which apply to those under twenty-one. Then there is the legal matter of emancipation which removes minors from parental control. The best example of this occurs when a minor marries or goes into the military service.

The powers to make decisions about children are distributed among the family, the state, and the child. Children generally have less liberty than adults, but they also have special rights. This was brought about primarily by laws which, starting in 1898, established special courts for juveniles. These laws provide that up to a certain age (usually sixteen or seventeen depending on what each state legislature determines is appropriate) children are subject to the laws which apply to them in a special court called the juvenile court, or in some states the family court. In a general way, these courts are there to see that care, protection, and discipline are provided for children. Preferably they should receive this in their own homes, but when they must be removed from their homes they should receive care as nearly as possible equivalent to that which they should have received at home.

When a juvenile violates a criminal law, which applies to all persons, he/she is considered to be delinquent. In these cases the purpose of the juvenile court is considered to be primarily rehabilitative. But the power of the court is very broad. The court may send the child back home or place him/her under supervision of a juvenile worker, or in a foster or group home, or in an institution. In the juvenile court, unlike the criminal court, there are no fixed terms of imprisonment. The court has very broad discretion and may retain control as long as it is considered necessary to provide treatment, but not longer than the twenty-first birthday.

In evaluating the so called "advantages" of the juvenile court over the criminal court we should not overlook the effectiveness of rehabilitative treatment and the length of time a juvenile may be required to undergo treatment, during which time his/her liberty is being restrained.

The matter of delinquency is only one aspect of the juvenile court's function. Of equal or greater importance is the power of that court to perform, on behalf of the state, the function of *parens patriae*. *Parens patriae* literally means "parent of the country" and in its original usage referred to the King of England in his capacity as the father protector or guardian for those persons who were under some disability such as being orphaned, insane, or under the age of majority. In the United States we substitute the state for king, and thus the state becomes the protector of children. In this capacity the state acts primarily through the juvenile court. When it is brought to the juvenile court's attention that parents have failed to care properly for their children, that court has the power to remove the children from their parents or, in extreme situations, to declare that the rights of parents are terminated and place the child with others who then can become the legal parents.

It is important to know that there are special laws that apply exclusively to young people. Since JUVENILE PROBLEMS AND LAW is written for the special purpose of introducing young people to "their law" it offers them the knowledge of what the law expects from them and enables them to assume their proper responsibilities in our society.

Noah Weinstein*

*Retired Circuit Judge, St. Louis County, Missouri, formerly Judge of the Juvenile Court of St. Louis County; faculty member, National College of Juvenile Justice; Saint Louis University, School of Social Service; Washington University, School of Social Work.

JUVENILE
PROBLEMS
AND

Students:

Juvenile Problems and Law was written for two reasons. One is to give you an opportunity to learn more about what you can do to help solve your own problems. Through different activities, role plays, and projects, the book will help you develop your skills as a problem solver. You will also have opportunities to experience helping others with their problems.

Some of your problems can be dealt with by you alone. Some you may need help in solving. However, if you take the responsibility for dealing with your problems, the juvenile court may never have to deal with them.

The second reason for writing this book was to tell the story of the juvenile court, how it began and how it functions today. Many people are concerned about today's juvenile court. There are serious questions being asked about how to deal with juvenile crime. We would like you to understand the problems of trying to work out effective and fair ways of treating young people in the legal system. If you understand the problems, you may want to get involved in working toward solutions.

Sincerely,
Linda Riekes
Sally Mahe Ackerly

Table of Contents

Juvenile Problems and Law

LAW IN ACTION SERIES
Second Edition

SECTION I   PROBLEM SOLVING
SOLVING PROBLEMS

Lesson 1

Objective: **Students will discuss their own attitudes about taking responsibility to solve problems.**

Students will be able to identify at least two ways of handling problems.

Here is a picture of students interviewing a juvenile court judge.

"I've been a juvenile judge for some time and have seen many different types of problems young people have. I think that it is important for young people to learn how to take more responsibility for themselves. A goal in any book about juvenile problems and law should be to help young people handle problems before they have to come to the courts or get into trouble with the law."

Do you agree with this person's opinion? State your reasons for agreeing or disagreeing.

How are Problems Solved?

PROBLEM SOLVING

I HAVE A PROBLEM TO SOLVE, BUT HOW? WHAT CAN I DO?

TIME PASSED...

I'VE GOT IT!

SNAP!

Do you think people really solve their problems the way this boy did? Explain your answer.

People go about solving problems in different ways. Complete each sentence below with a statement about how you think that person should handle the problem. Discuss your suggestions in class. For each problem list the four solutions the class decides are best.

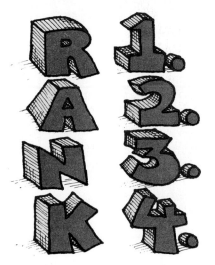

Rank the four solutions you picked in order, placing the one you think is the very best as number one and so on. Be sure to give reasons why you think those solutions are the best.

I'm getting horrible grades in school. I'm going to_____

_____

_____

I can't get along with my sister. I'm going to_____

_____

_____

There is trash messing up our neighborhood. I'm going to___

_____

_____

_____

You may run into problems that are too big for you to handle or that are out of your control. When facing a complex problem it's difficult to know what you can do about the problem, if anything. But even with a very complex problem the way you decide to respond to it can make things better or worse for you and for other people.

In which of these examples do you think the person stating the problem could do something about it? Explain your answer.

1. "If only I were not so fat I would have more friends."
2. "If only I could skip math class I would do well in school."

TAKING RESPONSIBILITY— Y.E.L. HOUSE

Objective: **Students will be able to define what being responsible means to them.**

Students will be able to identify and apply four steps used in problem solving.

The following story is true. It is about three young people who took responsibility to help other people with problems.

Y.E.L.

Linda Newmann, Peter Baker, and Curtis Banks were good friends who were always getting into trouble at school and in their community. They knew the police officer in their area by name. They were known as troublemakers at school and were frequent visitors to the principal's office. Each had been taken into juvenile court.

All of their friends called Linda, Peter and Curtis the "experts" in knowing what to do when you got into trouble. Kids who were in trouble came to them to ask for advice. Some of the problems the three heard about were really serious.

They knew the problems were too big for them to handle. None of them wanted to go to the juvenile officer or to the school principal for help. They thought there ought to be a place where young people like themselves could go to get help. Curtis really liked his probation counselor at the juvenile court. He told the counselor of the idea to have a "help center" where kids would not be afraid to go for help. Curtis, Linda, and Peter believed the center should be run mainly by kids. They wanted the adults to help, but wanted kids to be responsible for making the rules.

After a lot of talking, planning, and hard work they got their help center started. They named it Y.E.L. (Youth Emergency League). Soon kids with many different kinds of problems were in touch with the center.

Questions:

1. How did Linda, Peter, and Curtis take responsibility for solving a problem?

2. Explain in your own words what you think it means to be responsible, or to take responsibility for someone or something.

3. Do you know of any help centers in your community that try to assist young people with problems? Where are they located? What do they do? Are they used by young people? If not, why aren't they?

To find out more about help centers for young people in your area see the Community Involvement Project on page 9.

Now, on to find out about the steps in problem solving.

Everyone has problems at one time or another. Sometimes people don't try to solve their problems because they don't want to, don't know how, or perhaps are waiting for someone else to solve them. One way to get better at solving problems is through practice. There are certain skills you can learn to become better at solving problems. Here are four basic steps to follow:

1. Make sure you know what the problem is.

2. Ask yourself if you really care about solving it.

3. Think of different things you could do to solve it.

4. Choose one thing to do and do it. Look back to see if it really helped.

Pretend that are the person with the following problems.

Read each problem carefully. Then follow the four steps to try to solve each problem.

 1. Describe the problem.

 2. If you had this problem, would you really care about solving it. Explain your answer.

 3. What ways can you think of to do something about this problem? Make a list of the possible solutions.

 4. Choose one thing to do. Explain why you think this is the best action to take.

Problem 1

"I'm never going back to school. Just because I'm the biggest in my class that teacher is always picking on me. She asks me to carry books, move furniture, or carry movie equipment. I know I'm not a great student, but she takes advantage of me. I'm never carrying anything else, ever! I'm not going back to that class."

Problem 2

"I used to take drugs with my friends. I got messed up bad a few times and decided not to use any more drugs. I still like my friends though, but they don't like me because they say I'm a goody-goody. I don't know what to do."

Problem 3

"I'm fourteen. I hate my grand-father who is my guardian. He makes me do all the housework and cooking. For Christmas he threw me a pack of gum and said, 'Merry Christmas.' That was my present. I want to run away but I'm kind of afraid."

DO YOU KNOW WHAT KIND OF HELP CENTERS FOR YOUTH THERE ARE IN YOUR COMMUNITY?

Often there are help centers in the community, but people don't know about them. You can help yourself and others learn about help centers by conducting a survey to discover what kinds of help centers for young people there are in your community.

Divide the class into four groups. Each group could take a different type of organization in the area to see if they have help centers.

Group I	Group II	Group III	Group IV
Survey help centers run by religious organizations.	Survey help centers run by city or state government.	Survey help centers run by the juvenile court.	Survey help centers run by neighborhood groups.

What kind of services does your help center include?
What age people does your center serve?
Where is the center located and what hours is it open?
Who staffs the center?
Must people make an appointment?
Is there any fee involved?
What are the center's rules?
Do you have a pamphlet about the center? If not, would a pamphlet be helpful?

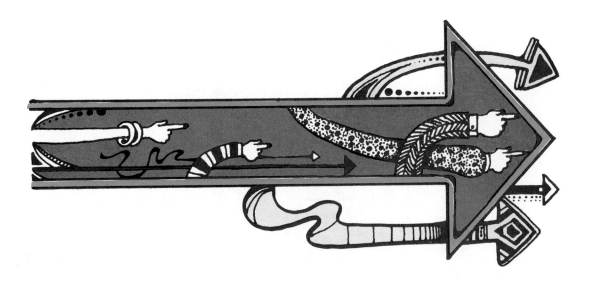

If any of the help centers would like a pamphlet telling about the services of the center or if they would like a new version of their old pamphlet, the group might want to design a new pamphlet for them. Or, the class as a whole might design a report on ALL the youth help centers in your community. Each group would offer the information gained from their interviews. This information could be organized and put together in one report which would inform people in your community. Remember to design your pamphlet or report so that it is appealing and easy to read. It is also important that your information be correct.

A well-written pamphlet or report could be very useful to the help centers. You could also distribute them at school PTA meetings so that parents, too, would know about the centers.

COUNSELING TRAINING

Objective: **Students will be able to identify six basic counseling skills.**

Students will be able to practice applying basic counseling skills.

The Y.E.L. staff decided they needed some training in counseling (helping people solve problems). They got training from professional counselors at the juvenile court. Here are some of the counseling skills they learned.

1. LISTENING

Learning to listen sounds easy but there is more to it than having good ears! See how well you listen . . .

Choose partners. You have one minute to find out as much as possible about your partner (how many in family? what they like to do after school? do they have pets? where do they live? have they ever travelled anywhere?). Then, your partner has one minute to ask you questions about yourself. At the end of two minutes, share all the information you have learned about your partner with the rest of the class. How well did you listen?

Have two people go to the front of the room. Have one person describe his/her neighborhood in three sentences. Then have the other person "paraphrase"—repeat what the person said in other words. Did the person paraphrasing give the correct meaning? Try several pairs. Let each person paraphrase the other. How well did people listen?

2. ASKING QUESTIONS

Basically, a counselor should know as much information about the problem as possible. For example:

—What exactly happened?

—How does the person with the problem feel about it? Does he or she think it is a problem?

—Besides the person with the problem, who else is involved? How might they view the situation?

Here is a problem told to a counselor. There are five questions the counselor asked. Mark which questions you think are helpful ones to ask and which ones you think are not helpful questions. Explain why.

"I have a problem with school work. Last term I failed almost everything. I just got my report card and I feel so dumb. Mom is going to kill me."

1. Do you think you worked as hard as you could last term?
2. Have you talked to any of your teachers about your grades?
3. Do you watch TV everyday?
4. What do you think you can do to do better next term?
5. Do you like peanut butter sandwiches?

3. DEVELOPING EMPATHY

Empathy means letting the other person know you understand what her/his problem is and how she/he feels.

A good counselor lets people know she/he cares about the person. Caring/interest can be shown by facial expressions, by the way one sits, and by the way the counselor responds to the person. Try this—

Think of a feeling like:

fear
anger
boredom
happy
sad
interested
I like you
depression
not interested
I'm better than you are
I care about you

Act out this feeling <u>without saying anything.</u> Show this feeling by facial expression and how you hold your body. See if the class can guess what feeling you are trying to express.

4. BUILDING TRUST

A helpful counselor must be able to be trusted not to tell others about a person's problems. It is very important that the person be able to trust you. He/she must know that the counselor will never tell anyone what he/she has talked about.

What does trust mean? Could you trust someone to be on time if that person was usually late to every meeting with you? Could you trust someone with an important secret if that person told everybody your business?

5. **HELPING A PERSON LOOK FOR ALTERNATIVES**
   Often people with a problem can think up different things
   they can do about it without being told what to do.
   A good counselor <u>helps</u> people find <u>alternatives</u>—different
   possible ways they might go about handling their
   problems.

For most problems there are different things a person can do
about them. Sometimes, the person with the problem can
think up alternatives alone; sometimes the person with the
problem needs someone like a counselor to give advice.

WHICH OF THESE DOORS WILL YOU CHOOSE ?

6. **FOLLOWING UP TO SEE IF THE PROBLEM IS
   IMPROVING**
   A helpful counselor makes sure he/she talks to the person
   again after the person has had a chance to try to handle
   the problem. A counselor can help a person see if what
   he/she is doing about the problem is really working or
   not.

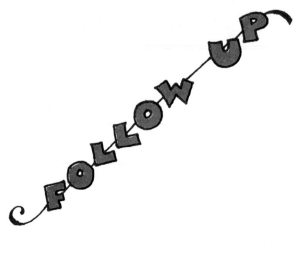

Practice your new skills in counseling by role playing the three stories in Lesson 1. One person should take the role of the person with the problem, and one person should act as the counselor. At the end of each role play, the counselor should explain how to handle basic skill 6—Follow-up. What would the follow-up be?

The rest of the group should observe the role plays carefully. Then they could use the following checklist to see how well the counselors put their skills into practice.

16

Observer Checklist: Mark how helpful you think the counselor was for each of the problems.

1. **LISTENING**
☐ very helpful ☐ helpful ☐ not very helpful

Give one example of how the counselor showed how well he/she could listen.

_____

2. **ASKING QUESTIONS**
☐ very helpful ☐ helpful ☐ not very helpful

Give one example of how the counselor showed how well he/she could ask questions.

_____

3. **DEVELOPING EMPATHY**
☐ very helpful ☐ helpful ☐ not very helpful

Give one example of how the counselor showed how well he/she indicated empathy.

_____

4. **BUILDING TRUST**
☐ very helpful ☐ helpful ☐ not very helpful

Give one example of how the counselor gave the feeling of being able to be trusted.

_____

5. **LOOKING FOR ALTERNATIVES**
☐ very helpful ☐ helpful ☐ not very helpful

Give one example of how the counselor helped look for alternatives.

_____

6. **FOLLOWING UP**
☐ very helpful ☐ helpful ☐ not very helpful

Give one example of how well the counselor thought about following up.

_____

PUTTING YOURSELF IN THE OTHER PERSON'S SHOES

Objective: Students will be able to discuss a problem from different viewpoints.

Students will be able to develop alternative solutions to two problems given.

In attempting to deal with your own problems or someone else's, it is helpful to put yourself in the other person's shoes.

Look at the situation from a point of view other than your own.

For example:

When a fight broke out on the school yard, some students thought Larry was to blame for starting it, and just as many students thought Phil had started the fight. Often different people see the same situation from a different point of view.

Here is another example:

Suppose children and parents disagree over what time the children should go to bed. One child will see the problem from his/her point of view and he might say, "I'm ten years old and should not have to go to bed at the same time my 8-year-old sister does."

His mother might see the problem from a different point of view and say, "The children are so active all day and use up so much energy, they both need all the sleep they can get. With both of us working everyday, their father and I need some quiet time for ourselves. His father might say, "I agree with my wife." And the 8-year-old sister might say, "I want to go to bed when by brother does and not before!"

How many points of view are represented here? What are they?

PRETEND YOU ARE ON THE STAFF AT Y.E.L. HOUSE AND MUST HANDLE THE FOLLOWING PROBLEMS.

These stories present different sides of a problem. The first story deals with a mother and son. The second story deals with a student and a teacher. Put your problem-solving and counseling skills to work in trying to help these people handle their problems.

1. Discuss these stories in groups and answer the questions which follow each story.

2. Share your suggestions for ways to help with the rest of the class.

3. After you have discussed these stories, you might want to role play a scene of a Y.E.L. staff person handling the cases according to your group's suggestions.

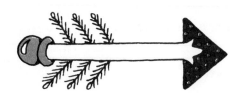

STORY 1

Tony

I am 14 years old. I want to leave home 'cause my mother is impossible to live with. She thinks she can dish out all the orders . . . tell me when to be home and always asks me about who my friends are. My mother is always yelling at me and I yell back. I don't need her telling me what to do. I want to run and start living my own life.

Tony's mother

Tony gets angry quickly. I want what's best for him. I hear of so many problems with drinking, drugs, and trouble with police that children his age get involved with, t causes me to worry. I realize he vants more freedom. I do care vhether or not he gets into trouble. It's been hard for me to handle him ever since his father died. I don't know exactly when it's best to leave him on his own and when to force him to obey my rules; but I cannot stand it when he talks back and treats me with no respect. If only we could talk without him losing his temper.

What are Tony's feelings?

What is the problem as Tony sees it?

What are his mother's feelings?

What is the problem as his mother sees it?

What suggestions can you make that might help Tony and his mother handle their problem?

Note to students: This story, like all stories in the book, is based on a real-life situation. Though the photo is of Tony and his mother, you can role play the same story with Tammy and her mother.

STORY 2

Mr. Green

At first Laurel seemed bored in class. I could tell she didn't like English. When we talked about it, she said she didn't think she was good in English, so she didn't try.

After a while in my class, she seemed to like English better. Her papers improved greatly. I was very pleased with her progress and told her so. I decided to give her a B for the course. I wanted to be fair to all the students in the class. I have a standard of what I consider A work to be. Some of the students met my standards and got an A. Laurel did not meet these standards. I didn't think it was fair to give her an A, even though I was happy with her progress.

Laurel

When I started Mr. Green's English course, I hated English. I had only gotten D's from most of my other teachers. Mr. Green was nice and talked to me a lot about interesting things in English. I started doing the assignments and Mr. Green kept telling me how pleased he was with my improvement. I was happy, too, and thought for sure I would get an A for the course. I'm angry now because he only gave me a B, and I think I deserved an A! I did all that work! He makes me so mad, I don't feel like talking to him again.

What was Mr. Green's position about giving Laurel an A?

Do you think it was a hard decision for him to make?

What was Laurel's point of view?

How did she feel when she received a B?

What are some ways that Laurel and Mr. Green might deal with this problem?

Take what you are learning in the classroom and put it to use in your community!

Tackle a problem at your school!

Here are steps to follow:

1. Discuss different problems at your school and decide on a problem that most people in your class think you could do something about.

2. Make sure that most people in your class really care about the problem and want to do something about it—not just talk about it.

3. Work together as a class to think up possible ways to work on this problem. Discuss which <u>alternatives</u> might work. What would it take to make them work.

4. Write down <u>a plan of action</u>. What jobs will people in the class have to do in order to carry out the plan of action. (Will some students talk to the principal? Will some students make posters?)

5. GET TO WORK!!!

6. Think about what happened. What was the result of your work? Was it a good plan? How would you do it differently if you had another chance?

REACHING A DECISION

Objectives: Students will be able to understand the decision-making process.

Students will be able to explain the meaning of due process of law.

The Y.E.L. House also took in young people who were involved with the juvenile court. Often young people stayed at Y.E.L. House several days while they waited for their hearing in juvenile court.

Two people under 18 and two adults make up the Board of Directors at Y.E.L. House. The Board made a rule that no alcohol or hard drugs could be used by anyone who stayed at Y.E.L. House. This was considered an important rule so that Y.E.L. House would not get a bad reputation in the neighborhood as a hangout for drug users.

James, a fourteen year old boy, had been staying at Y.E.L. House for one week instead of staying at the detention center* at the juvenile court. He was waiting to have his juvenile hearing* for shoplifting.

A staff person saw James out on the roof and saw some beer cans by his feet. The staff person asked if he had been drinking beer. James said, "No, the cans were just out on the roof." The staff person was sure he smelled beer on James' breath. The staff person reported the incident to the Board of Directors.

The Board of Directors had to reach a decision about James. First, they had to decide if he really had been drinking. Second, they had to decide what to do with him, if anything.

*Look up words in glossary.

Divide your class into groups. Each group should work together to handle this case. In every group there should be one student who role-plays James, one who role-plays the Y.E.L. staff person, and four students who role-play the four Board members at Y.E.L. House.

Your job is to reach two decisions.

1. Did James really break the rules about drinking at Y.E.L. House?

2. What should happen to him, if anything?

After you have reached these decisions, the group should work together to complete this form.

JAMES

STAFF MEMBER AT YEL

BOARD MEMBERS AT YEL

Decision 1

WHAT DID YOU DECIDE?

Did you find James guilty of breaking the drinking rule at Y.E.L. House?   Yes   No

Give the reasons for your decision. _____

_____

HOW DID YOU DECIDE?

—Did James present his story?   Yes   No

—Did the staff person who saw him present his story? Yes   No

—Did all the Board members ask questions during the discussion?   Yes   No

—What other things did you do in order to reach your decision? _____

_____

—Do you think the way you made your decision about James' guilt or innocence was fair? Yes   No

Explain   why _____

_____

_____

Decision 2

WHAT DID YOU DECIDE?

What did you decide to do with James?

—Send him back to detention at the juvenile court?
Yes   No

—Give him some extra work to do around Y.E.L. House?   Yes   No

—Give him a warning about what would happen if he did it again?   Yes   No

—Nothing?   Yes   No

—Other? _____

Give a reason for the decision you made. _____

_____

_____

HOW DID YOU DECIDE?

—Did James have anything to say about what should happen to him?   Yes   No

—Did any of the Board members disagree about what should happen to him?   Yes   No

—Did you reach a decision about what should happen to him by voting?   Yes   No

—Did one person decide what should happen to him and talk everyone else into seeing it that way?
Yes   No

—What other things did you do to reach your decision?

_____

_____

Do you think the way you make your decision about what should happen to James was fair?
Yes   No

Explain why. _____

_____

_____

Being treated fairly has to do with not only <u>what decision is made</u> but also <u>how that decision is made</u>. The set of steps people go through to reach a decision is called a

When a **process** involves the law, and the police, lawyers, judges or probation officers assist in reaching a decision, it is called the legal process.

In this process certain rules of law are applied in arriving at a decision. For example, the sixth amendment of the United States Constitution says that people have a right to a fair and speedy trial. That is a rule of law. A judge must decide which rules of law apply to each case. These rules are intended to make sure that people who come before the court are treated fairly and equally.

Think of some of the laws you know about already that are supposed to make sure people get fair treatment in courts. For example, there is a rule of law that says the accused person has the right to tell her/his side of the story if she/he wants to.

_____   _____

_____   _____

_____   _____

_____   _____

_____   _____

_____   _____

The United States Constitution is the highest law in the land. The fourteenth amendment to the United States Constitution says that all people have the right to be treated fairly in a legal procedure. This amendment calls this right to fair treatment "due process of law."

The fourteenth amendment states in part:
>   ".   .   .   nor shall any state deprive any person of life, liberty, or property without due process of law."

Due process means:
- —looking at the facts that can be proven, rather than making judgments on something you hear.
- —having an attorney represent you.
- —having all sides of a story brought out.
- —being told of the offense you are charged with.
- —having the punishment fit the crime.

.   .   .   And it has come to mean much more   .   .   .
Courts continue to interpret the constitution and laws and lawmakers continue to make new laws concerning what fair treatment means.

THE CASE OF GERALD GAULT

Objective: Students will be able to explain what the constitutional right to due process means for juveniles.

Today, young people under a certain age (it varies from state to state) are by law considered juveniles. There are juvenile courts set up to handle their cases. There are laws that state what due process rights young people have when they come before the juvenile court. Juveniles did not always have these due process rights. For a long time these safeguards applied only to adult criminal trials. The juvenile court started with the idea that young people did not need the same safeguards that an adult in a criminal case would need. Juvenile court had very informal hearings. It was thought that juveniles would be better off to have an informal hearing rather than a formal legal procedure. Then in 1967 the United States Supreme Court, the highest court in the country, was asked to make a decision regarding the rights of juveniles in the case of a fifteen-year-old boy named Gerald Gault.

HERE IS THE STORY

List the things that happened during this legal process that you think are unfair.

_____   _____

_____   _____

_____   _____

Something did happen in the case of Gerald Gault. After he went to the State Training School his parents went to a lawyer and explained everything that had happened to Gerald. The lawyer agreed that if what the Gaults said was true Gerald had not been given fair treatment. He had been denied "due process of law."

Since Arizona law at that time did not allow cases involving juveniles to be taken to a higher court, the lawyer asked the state court in Arizona for a writ of habeas corpus. (A writ of habeas corpus is a procedure by which people already in prison can ask to have their case heard in a higher court.) He argued that the Juvenile Code of Arizona went against the due process clause of the fourteenth amendment. The case was finally heard by the United States Supreme Court. The Supreme Court ruled in favor of Gerald Gault.

• In the Gault case the Supreme Court ruled that juveniles who are accused of offenses for which they could be sent to an institution must have the following rights:

1. **Right to notice of charges**— Being told exactly what you are accused of long enough in advance of your hearing to be able to prepare your case.

2. **Right to counsel**—Being told you have a right to a lawyer, that if you don't have enough money to pay, the court must appoint a lawyer for you.

3. **Right to confrontation and cross-examination**—Being able to hear the testimony of the witnesses and of your accusers. Testimony is the information a witness gives under oath. Cross-examination means that the accused or the lawyer for the accused has the chance to ask the witness questions.

4. **Privilege against self-incrimination**—Being told you have a right to remain silent because anything you say might be used against you.

• In later cases the courts have since ruled that an accused juvenile must have the right to:

A transcript of the proceedings— Having every word said at your hearing written down.

An appellate review—Having the right to ask to have your case heard by a higher court if you wish to have the decision reached in the first hearing reversed.

Before 1967 young people were not given the due process rights listed on page 30. What happened to Gerald Gault could have happened to other young people.

After 1967 courts and police officers dealing with juveniles had to follow the decision made by the Supreme Court in Gerald Gault's case. They have to make sure that young persons coming to the juvenile court are protected by the due process safeguards. These safeguards have developed since 1967.

Now draw your own cartoon story of the case of Gerald Gault as it might happen today. Be certain to include the specific rights of the young person that the court must uphold.

THE CASE OF GERALD GAULT AS IT MIGHT HAVE HAPPENED AFTER THE 1967 SUPREME COURT DECISION ACCORDING TO _____
your name

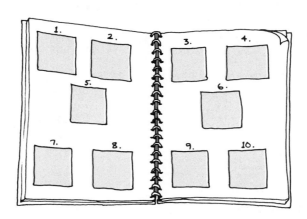

The case of Gerald Gault made important changes in the legal process used to handle young people who came before the juvenile courts. The juvenile court is still undergoing changes. It may be very different six years from now. How it changes depends upon people—people who care enough to learn about the court and to work for changes.

The next section in this book deals with how the juvenile court started and how it operates today.   There is much discussion today about the juvenile court.

Courts Fail To Slow Juvenile Crime, Study Says

NEW YORK (UPI) — The justice system has not stemmed the steady increase in violent crimes committed by youths, a new study reported Saturday.

The arrest rate for such crimes tripled between 1960 and 1975.

The study was prepared for the Ford Foundation by New York's Vera Institute, a non-profit research group. It said that little is known as to why certain juveniles commit violent crimes, and it called for more studies to resolve the point.

Perhaps as ma... juveniles hav... they are 18, th...

lice made 2.1 million arrests of youths between the ages of 7 and 18.

Most of the arrests were for minor offenses, but 4 percent of the arrests were for crimes against persons such as assault, robbery, homicide and rape, the report said. The greatest increases in juvenile crime have occurred in...

Paul ...

Kennedy: Tougher Courts Needed For Juveniles

NEW YORK (AP) — Sen. Edward M. Kennedy says states should get tough with violent juveniles, bringing them to trial in adult ...d sentencing them to "sig-...

...dent juve-...

that probation or training school appeared "to have little or no constructive impact on subsequent criminal behavior."

On the other ... some ...

Kennedy takes over next year as chairman of the Senate Judiciary Committee, which handles most federal anti-crime legislation. His hard line on juvenile crime surprised some listeners aware of the senator's liberal voting record.

Kennedy said the nature of the ...crime, rather than the defendant's ...uld determine which court ...

...ating the ...

High Court May Consider Juvenile Rights

By LYLE DENNISTON
1978, Washington Star

WASHINGTON
BEN CHANEY WAS JUST about 12 when he and his family learned how vicious the nation's struggle ... rights could be.

His brother James, 21, a ci... worker, had been spirited away ... Neshoba County jail in Phila... Miss., and was missing.

collector and two college students.

BEFORE GIVING that statement, he had been given "Miranda warnings" — that is he was told by police of his ri... silent and his ri...

"mentally disturbed" youth from home a...

lower-class or ... urban cen-... hey tend to ...have poor ... t likely ... y may ... w of ... ave ...

Seeks To Try Youth As Adult For Rape

A 13-year-old youth has been charged with raping a 73-year-old East St. Louis woman Monday night in her home. Clyde L. Kuehn, St. Clair County state's attorney, said he will seek to have the youth tried as an adult.

...Sgt. Gregory Cox said the youth broke into the ...dow forced her husband, ...

went to a neighbor's home to summon police, who caught the intruder, Cox said.

The woman was treated at St. Mary's Hospital in East St. Louis.

Kuehn said that normally a youth cannot be charged even under the juvenile code until he is 13. But he said ...th should be tried as an adult because he has an ...

Youth violence: More to it than headlines say

By JERRY SCHWARTZ
Associated Press Writer

NEW YORK — Sensational crimes by adolescents steal headlines and prompt public alarm, but it's the more common violent crimes — assault and robbery — that have fueled a dramatic increase in the juvenile crime rate, according to a new report.

"The public is extremely impatient for a solution to this problem," but solutions are not apparent and the problem is misunderstood, said Paul A. Strasburg, author of "Violent Delinquents," a report to the Ford Foundation by the Vera Institute of Justice.

THE INSTITUTE is a non-profit organization that conducts research and demonstration projects aimed at improving the criminal justice system and rehabilitating offenders.

In the report released Saturday, Strasburg said he found that:

—Race is not an important factor in youth violence, but location, school failure and family breakups are important.

—A Vera Institute study of the seriousness of violent crimes found that on the average, 13-year-olds committed the most serious crimes compared to the remainder of the study group — ages 13 to 18. Strasburg concluded that "younger and younger kids are competing with their older siblings for the title of who's the most violent."

—THE MOST VIOLENT delinquents are refused entry to programs that might help them because they are feared by the program organizers. Instead, they are neglected and forced to spend their young lives in work schools and other facilities.

Strasburg said that despite a recent spate of sensational violent crimes by juveniles, little research has been done on "the serious, hard-core, violent delinquent."

"Media attention to murders, rapes, and other heinous crimes involving juveniles has created a belief, accurate or not, that today's delinquents are more ruthless, more dangerous than their predecessors in earlier years," the report said.

The truth is hard to pinpoint, according to the report. Arrests for juvenile violent crimes jumped 231.5 percent between 1960 and 1975, with a slight decrease since 1975. Strasburg estimated that as many as one-third of America's young have police records by age 18.

BUT THE REPORT also notes that violent repeaters are not common among

juveniles, with perhaps 3 to 5 percent of youths arrested having been arrested more than once for violent offenses. The most frequent violent offense committed by juveniles is simple assault; the next most common serious violent crime is robbery, followed by serious assault.

Murder and sex attacks account for less than 1 percent of all crimes committed by juveniles, compared with 3 percent for adults.

"We have to be careful not to shoot a cannon to kill a fly," Strasburg said. "The question is, 'what are we going to do about robbers' — not 'what are we going to do about killers.'"

Strasburg also reported that "youth violence is, by and large, an urban phenomenon," although suburban youth violence is growing at a faster rate than urban violence.

People are asking:

Does it really help young people?

Is it more fair to young people than an adult court?

Is it fair to the rest of society?

Should there even be a separate court to handle juvenile cases?

Many people have never heard of the Gault case and don't really know what this legal process is all about. As a class you might write a script for a skit about the Gault case. You could act out the story from start to finish. If you need more facts for your story, ask a law student, a lawyer, or someone who knows how to use a law library to find the case. You can follow the actual story fact-by-fact as it appears in the reported case.

Do your presentation for an audience—perhaps another class or a parent group. You might make a video-tape of the story if your school has a video-tape machine.

Objective: Students will be able to define a list of words introduced in Section I.

You have already seen these words in the previous lessons. Do you know the meaning of them right now? Try to match each of these words with its proper definition.

juvenile

a. a person who helps to solve other people's problems, an advisor

counselor

b. a choice between two or more possibilities

due process

c. fair treatment under the law

fourteenth amendment

d. a young person, not yet adult

alternative

e. part of the United States Constitution which states the right to due process of law

Check your work by looking up each of these words in the glossary. Write the correct definition of any word you missed. Make sure you know the meaning of each word before going on.

NEWSBULLETIN REVIEW—SECTION I

Objective: Students will be able to answer questions on a class test about information presented in Section I.

Note to students: This lesson is a review quiz. You can use it to check how much you have learned so far about problem solving and juvenile law. Some classes have turned these reviews into newsbulletins. When your answers get printed in a newsbulletin, they help other people learn what you have learned.

The next page gives you an idea of what the finished newsbulletin might look like. It was done by another class. Take a look. . . .

THE NOW EXPLOSION

EDITORIAL

Do you think young people under 17 should be treated differently for committing illegal acts?

Yes, but the age should be fifteen not seventeen. Sixteen and seventeen-year-olds should be treated like adults. They are old enough to have thought through their actions.

Savannah L.

No, people must be responsible for their actions at any age. Young people can't say "Oh, I'm too young to think about that."

Darion

No, because if you can commit a crime, you can take the punishment like an adult.

Mickey N.

CROSSWORD PUZZLE: Susan

CARTOON

John saw a strange boy knock down his neighbor and steal her purse. What would you do if you were John?

Cheryl

Be certain that you really put yourself in the other person's shoes. Empathy means that you try to see the other person's side. It is important because if you can do that the person can trust you and your opinion.

Sophie

ADVICE COLUMN

Of the six basic skills in counseling which one do you think is most important?

It is very difficult to know what to say. The six skills in the book are very important. It is important to know all the alternatives you can for that person. Having alternatives gives the person who is being counselled hope.

Adam

NEWSBULLETIN REVIEW

Advice Column

Where could a young person with a problem go for help in your community? Give two reasons for naming this place or person.

Gerald Gault

In the Gerald Gault case the United States Supreme Court ruled to grant juveniles certain rights. Explain three of these rights in your own words.

1. _____

_____

2. _____

_____

3. _____

_____

Editorial

What does it mean to take responsibility for yourself? Give one example.

What does it mean to take responsibility for others? Give one example.

Crossword Puzzle

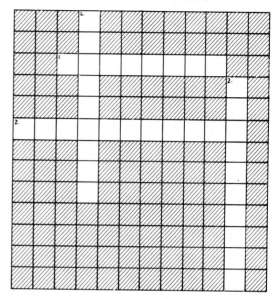

Down:

1. An advisor
2. Fair treatment under the law.

Across:

1. A young person who is not yet an adult.
2. A choice between two or more possibilities.

Helpful Hints

List the four steps in problem solving.

 1.

 2.

 3.

 4.

SECTION II JUVENILE COURT
JUVENILE COURT AND LAW—
THE BEGINNING

Objective: Students will be able to explain the theory behind the establishment of the juvenile court system.

Students will be able to state reasons for laws that treat young people differently than adults.

Students will be able to give their opinions concerning special laws that apply to young people.

There have not always been juvenile courts. . . .

The time is 1895. How long ago was that?

Can you imagine what life was like then? Pretend you were alive in 1895. Besides not having cars and TV, what else would you <u>not</u> have?

_____   _____

_____   _____

_____   _____

Do the things you have now that you did not have in 1895 help society? Explain how these things help society or how they might cause problems for society. (For example, cars make it easy to travel but they cause pollution.)

In 1895 there were no juvenile courts or special jails for young people. Any child over seven who broke the law could be sent to adult jail. Most young people were treated like adults when they went to court.

Some people strongly disagreed with the way young people were treated. One man put it this way: "Does clubbing a person make him better? Children need care, not harsh punishment!"

In the late 1890s, a small group of people who wanted to change the law as it concerned young people met in Chicago. They drew up ideas for special courts just for juveniles. The purpose of these special courts would be to HELP rather than PUNISH the young person. This concept was made law by the legislature and was adopted as a juvenile code in Illinois in 1899. Part of this code says:

"Children as far as practicable . . . shall be treated not as criminals but as children in need of aid, encouragement, and guidance."

This was the first juvenile code, since then laws establishing a juvenile justice system have been adopted in every state.

In addition to a juvenile code, other laws have been passed which deal with young people. Some people feel that by limiting what a young person can do, these laws protect young people from harm. Some believe these laws protect young people from responsibility they are not ready to handle. Still others believe they limit a young person's actions unnecessarily or unfairly. Having laws that apply only to nonadults raises an important question for society to think about . . .

AT WHAT AGE AND UNDER WHAT CIRCUM-STANCES SHOULD A YOUNG PERSON BE TREATED AS AN ADULT?

On the next page you will find seven questions about special laws for young people. People who answer YES to the question should stand on one side of the room. People who answer NO to the question should stand on the opposite side of the room.

First, one person from the YES side gives his/her reasons for being on that side. Then, one person on the NO side must repeat what the person from the YES side said before giving his/her reasons for being on the NO side. Continue this way until everyone on each side has given a reason for his/her opinion.

Remember that listening is very important. You need to understand the other person's point of view.

DO YOU THINK THERE SHOULD BE LAWS THAT SAY:

1. People must be 16 to drive a car?

   YES because . . .   NO because . . .

2. People must be 18 years old to serve on juries?

   YES because . . .   NO because . . .

3. People must attend school until they are 16 years old?

   YES because . . .   NO because . . .

4. People under 18 cannot sign a contract?

   YES because . . .   NO because . . .

5. People under 18 may not vote in government elections?

   YES because . . .   NO because . . .

6. People under 15 or 16 cannot run away from home?

   YES because . . .   NO because . . .

7. People under 16 or 17 may not get married without their parents' consent?

   YES because . . .   NO because . . .

Note to students: Age requirements for all these laws vary from state to state.

Read All About It

On the preceding page is a list of laws which apply to young people. These laws may vary from state to state. By looking up the statutes (laws) for your state you will find what age is set by each law. You will also learn when each law was passed and perhaps why it was passed. The group which is going to do this project may ask the librarian to show them how to look up state statutes. Write a report on your findings.

JUVENILE COURTS AND ADULT COURTS

Objective: Students will be able to explain at least four differences between the adult criminal court and the juvenile court.

Be a Detective.

Search the next two pages for information you will need to answer the statements on this page.

After you find the answers you will have a better idea of the differences between juvenile courts and adult criminal courts.

ARE THESE STATEMENTS TRUE OR FALSE?

1. A young person who is 14 can never stand trial as an adult. _____

2. A juvenile court judge can give a juvenile a sentence of life in prison. _____

3. An adult's criminal record is destroyed once he or she has served time in a penal institution. _____

4. Adult criminal courts have dispositional hearings. _____

5. A juvenile hearing must be private and confidential. _____

There are major differences between the adult criminal courts and the juvenile courts. Here are some of them:

JUVENILE COURT   ADULT COURT

YEARS | 1 2 3 4 5 6 7 8 9 10 11 12 13 14 15 | 16 17 18 | 19 20 21 ➔ | YEARS

Handles young people who have:

—been abused or neglected by their families.

—broken a special law that applies only to young people, such as being truant from school or running away from home.

—broken criminal laws.

Holds a private, confidential fact-finding hearing (to establish what happened).

Holds a dispositional hearing (to decide what should be done).

Judge could give dispositional alternatives which include probation, placement in a foster care home, commitment to a group home or to a minimum or maximum security training school.

Most severe penalty: about a two-year term in a maximum security state institution for juveniles. But, a young person may be certified as an adult for committing a particular crime. When this happens the juvenile has to go through the adult court process.

Handles adults who have been accused of breaking criminal laws.

Holds a public trial.

Gives a sentence or penalty. Punishment can be a fine, probation, or imprisonment in a city jail, a state or federal prison.

Most severe penalty: life in prison or (in some states) capital punishment.

JUVENILE COURT   ADULT COURT

YEARS | 1 2 3 4 5 6 7 8 9 10 11 12 13 14 15 | 16 17 18 | 19 20 21 ————————▶ | YEARS

In theory, the main task of both lawyers is to work for the best interest of the young person and of society.

The state, the young person, his or her parents—each has a right to be represented by a lawyer.

Juvenile's attorney must see that the juvenile's rights are protected, and must present all evidence favorable to the young person's case. In many cases, the juvenile's guilt is not at issue (he or she may have admitted guilt) and so the attorney plays a greater role in the "dispositional hearing." The juvenile's attorney may consult with social service workers, psychologists, and others to determine the most satisfactory "disposition."

The juvenile court judge decides the facts of the case and the disposition. (Some states offer jury trials for juveniles.)

Record: a young person found to be delinquent receives a juvenile record. Most of this information is sealed when the young person is no longer considered a juvenile. However, a record of crimes committed remains. It can be used by a judge in an adult court when fixing a sentence.

In a criminal case, a prosecuting lawyer represents the public, and may be a state, county, or city attorney. He or she presents evidence and argues to prove that the crime was committed and the defendant committed it. If defendant is convicted, recommends a sentence which will most appropriately serve the public's interests.

Defense lawyer represents defendant. Must see that defendant's constitutional rights have not been violated. At the trial, presents evidence and argues to prove that defendant did not commit the crime. If defendant is found guilty, defense attorney brings to court's attention circumstances which would justify the minimum penalty.

A jury, or a judge without a jury, decides the case. The judge decides the sentence. In states which have capital punishment, a jury decides whether the death sentence should be given in cases involving capital offenses.

Record: a person convicted of a crime then has a criminal record which remains active during that person's lifetime.

DISCUSSING THE DIFFERENCES

The terms used to describe what happens in juvenile and adult criminal court are different.

Why do you think these different terms are used?

WORDS USED

In juvenile court a person:
—is <u>taken into custody</u>
—commits an <u>offense</u>
—has a <u>hearing</u>
—is found <u>delinquent</u>
—receives a <u>disposition</u>

Rank these items according to what you think the major purposes of the <u>juvenile court</u> should be:

to <u>help</u> the juvenile change his/her ways

to <u>protect</u> society from juveniles who break the law

to <u>punish</u> juveniles who break the law

to make sure a juvenile is <u>treated fairly</u> when he/she comes before the court

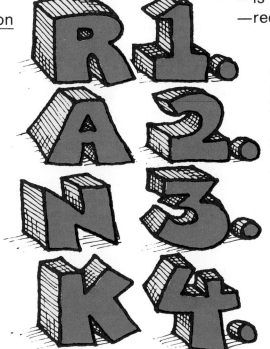

WORDS USED

In adult court a person:
—is <u>arrested</u>
—commits a <u>crime</u>
—has a <u>trial</u>
—is found <u>guilty</u>
—receives a <u>sentence</u>

Rank these items according to what you think the major purposes of the <u>adult</u> court should be:

to <u>help</u> the adult change his/her ways

to <u>protect</u> society from adults who break the law

to <u>punish</u> adults who break the law

to make sure an adult is <u>treated fairly</u> when she/he comes before the court

1. Did you rank the purposes for the juvenile court and adult criminal court exactly the same? If so, why do you think they should be the same?

2. Did you rank the purposes for the juvenile court and the adult criminal court differently? If so, explain the ways in which they are different and why you ranked them that way.

3. In your own words state the purpose of the juvenile court. State the main purpose of the adult criminal court.

JUVENILE COURT PROCESS

Objective: Students will be able to explain the basic steps involved in the juvenile court process.

In Lesson 5, "Reaching A Decision," it was explained that being treated fairly has to do not only with <u>what</u> decision is made about you, but also <u>how</u> that decision is made. The steps the juvenile court goes through to reach a decision about a juvenile is called a **process**. A juvenile who is accused of committing an offense becomes involved in the juvenile court process. There are certain rules of law that must be followed as part of this process to insure that the juvenile gets fair treatment. This is the safeguard called "right to due process of law" that is protected by the United States Constitution.

This lesson takes you through a juvenile court process. The "due process" steps apply to juvenile cases anywhere in the United States. However, juveniles are handled differently in other ways, depending upon the locality.

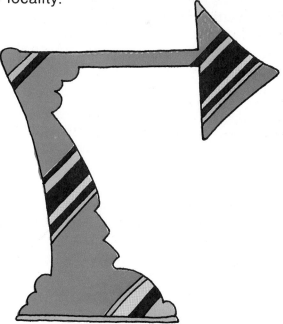

The Case: Frank Jones, age 14, was taken into custody by two juvenile police officers and accused of snatching a woman's purse. This is the story of what happened to him in juvenile court.

The Offense: A purse snatching

Purse snatching is usually considered robbery because it is the taking of property from a person by force or with violence. The offense may be simple robbery or, if a great deal of force is used or if the victim is severely injured, it may be considered "aggravated robbery." The amount of money taken does not affect what the offense is called; even if the purse snatcher gets only a few coins it is still robbery if force and violence are used. If the purse snatcher uses any kind of deadly weapon the offense is called "armed robbery" or "aggravated robbery."

Do you think the penalty for robbery and armed or aggravated robbery should be the same or different? Explain your reasons.

The victim gives the police officers a description of the purse snatcher.

With this information the two police officers stop a suspect, Frank Jones, who fits the description and who is walking nearby.

The police officers frisk for weapons. They ask the suspect his name, address, and age. A police officer reads Frank his rights and they then take him into custody. He's taken to juvenile court.

1) What rights does Frank have in this situation?
2) Do you think Frank was angry or scared? How should Frank act toward the police in this situation?

The police fill out a report about their contact with Frank Jones. A juvenile court "intake officer" talks to Frank. Frank does not have to answer questions about the offense. Frank calls his mother. At this time the intake officer may let Frank go home with his mother or may keep him in detention until his hearing.

In this case, the intake officer knows Frank because Frank has been charged with purse snatching before. He decides to hold Frank in detention until his first hearing. Detention is a place where juveniles are kept (detained) until their hearings. This is not part of a juvenile's punishment although they are locked in and cannot leave.

Do you think holding juveniles in detention before their case is decided is necessary? Under what circumstances should a juvenile be kept in detention?

A detention worker gives Frank a room. He must leave his clothes and things with the detention worker. He receives a T-shirt and jeans to wear. The length of time he spends in detention before a hearing may vary.

At the first (preliminary) hearing the juvenile court decides whether to keep Frank in detention until his second hearing or let him go home. In many states a juvenile is asked to plead guilty or not guilty at this hearing. A juvenile should have a lawyer present at this hearing. If a juvenile does not admit committing the offense (pleads not guilty), another hearing will be held at which the court will decide whether or not the juvenile committed the offense.

If a juvenile does admit committing the offense (pleads guilty to the charges) at this hearing, a dispositional hearing will be held, at which the court will decide what to do with the juvenile.

Frank says he did not steal the purse. The juvenile court lawyer must then prepare for the adjudicatory (fact-finding) hearing by trying to put together facts (evidence) to prove Frank committed the offense.

Frank's lawyer needs to check the facts that will support his argument that Frank did not commit the offense.

The hearing is usually scheduled within several weeks of the date the juvenile is taken into custody.

A juvenile court counselor talks with Frank and his mother to learn about Frank's life at school and at home. He or she will then write a report and present it to the judge before the hearing.

If you were the counselor what questions would you ask? How would those questions help you do your job as counselor?

The juvenile counselor's responsibility is to learn the special circumstances and background of each juvenile. The counselor must also review the different places where the juvenile might be sent. Based on knowledge of the juvenile and of the available juvenile correction resources, the counselor makes a recommendation to the judge.

At the adjudicatory hearing the juvenile court lawyer and Frank's lawyer present the evidence. They may ask witnesses to testify. (To tell the court the facts of the incident as they saw them). The judge will then decide whether or not Frank committed the purse snatching.

If Frank is found delinquent (guilty) he will then have a dispositional hearing. Often this hearing takes place on the same day as the adjudicatory hearing. The judge makes the final decision of what should happen to Frank. Before the hearing the judge reads the report and recommendation made by the juvenile counselor. The judge's decision is often influenced by this recommendation. Why do you think this is so?

This is the usual procedure a juvenile would follow. However, each juvenile court may vary the procedure in some way, or provide for additional "steps" in the procedure.

54

Note to students: Remember a "hearing" is really a "listening"—a time when all the information about a case is listened to.

Most juvenile courts have three hearings. The 2nd and 3rd hearings are usually on the same day.

Preliminary Hearing

1st Hearing

To decide whether or not the court will take custody of the juvenile; to decide whether or not the juvenile will be kept in detention or be released to the parents.

A juvenile has a right to be represented by a lawyer here, and the parents must be so notified. If they cannot afford a lawyer, one will be appointed by the court.

Adjudicatory Hearing

2nd Hearing

To find the facts; to decide whether or not the juvenile committed the offenses of which he or she stands accused.

A juvenile has a right to have a lawyer present here.

Dispositional Hearing

3rd Hearing

To decide what will be done with the delinquent juvenile.

A judge is often influenced in making a decision about what to do with a juvenile by the recommendation of the social worker or juvenile counselor who has worked with the juvenile.

A juvenile has a right to have a lawyer present here.

A very ambitious project might be to do a slide show about the juvenile court. You could include several different cases to show the many kinds of problems the juvenile court handles.

There are several ways you might go about getting the help needed in this project:

1) You might work with a group in your community that is particularly interested in juveniles. The group you work with could help you get the camera and slides needed to do a slide show. They could also assist you in contacting the juvenile court judge to ask his/her permission and cooperation in this activity.

2) You might work with a juvenile police officer and a juvenile court counselor. They could help you make certain your pictures and information were accurate. Perhaps you could get permission to stage your pictures in the court room (when it was not in use) and in the detention center.

3) If some members of your group are especially talented in art they may be able to draw some of the pictures for the slides. This would be cheaper than using film and could be very effective.

If your class has the use of a tape recorder you might want to tape a brief message to accompany each slide. The slide show could be shown to the parents' association and to other classes in your school. It could then be presented to the juvenile court.

JUVENILE COURT HEARING

Objective: **Students will be able to identify the job responsibilities of people involved in a juvenile hearing.**

Students will enact a hearing and analyze it as a legal way of resolving a human problem.

Juvenile delinquency cases are only one part of the juvenile court's work. Of equal importance is the power of the court to perform the function of "parens patriae" for the state. "Parens patriae" are Latin words which mean "parent of the country." In the U.S. it has come to mean the state's role as the protector of children.

Each state has laws against child abuse and neglect. The laws are slightly different in each state but the wording is similar to:

"a child is abused and neglected when the environment he or she lives in is harmful to the welfare of the child."

Read this account of how a juvenile court handled the case of Robbie and Danny Lloyd. Robbie and Danny may or may not have been victims of child abuse.

Their case will be decided at this hearing in which you will take part.

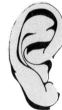

The Hearing

Juvenile Courts have two hearings to handle child abuse and neglect cases. The first hearing is the adjudicatory, or fact-finding, hearing. The lawyers ask the witnesses questions to bring the facts of the case before the court. The judge makes a decision. If the judge decides it is a case of child abuse or neglect, then the court has the power to do something about it.

The second hearing is the dispositional hearing. At this hearing the court decides what should be done. Usually a social worker who has studied the possible alternatives makes a recommendation to the judge. The lawyers can argue about this recommendation if they don't think it is fair. The judge makes the final decision. At this hearing there is another lawyer called the Attorney Ad Litem, or Guardian Ad Litem. This lawyer is appointed by the court to protect the child's interest during this hearing. (Ad litem means "at the trial" or "for the suit.") This lawyer's job is to make sure that what the court decides to do is in the best interest of the child.

59

THE CASE OF ROBBIE AND DANNY LLOYD

THE CASE OF
ROBBIE & DANNY LLOYD

JAN. 4 Child Abuse Hot Line Service receives call of possible child abuse concerning Robbie (age 7) and Danny Lloyd (age 2). Neighbor reports Robbie has asked her for food for himself and his little brother, Danny. Neighbor is concerned because he has seen the boys' mother leave the children home alone and stay away several hours. Neighbor reports Robbie looks skinny and sick and his hair, face, hands, and clothes are dirty. Child Abuse Hot Line volunteer reports this call to Division of Family Services.

JAN. 10 A social worker from Division of Family Services goes to the Lloyd's home. He finds no food in the home, heating only with space heaters, and no phone. Mrs. Lloyd says she only leaves the boys alone when she has to leave home and it's only happened once or twice. She said the boys' grandmother was supposed to babysit but never showed up. She says she brings in food every day for the boys and herself. The social worker asks if there is any way that Mrs. Lloyd needs help. Mrs. Lloyd says no. The social worker warns her not to leave her boys alone at home anymore.

FEB. 12 Child Abuse Hot Line Service receives another call from neighbor concerning Robbie and Danny Lloyd. Robbie has been over to ask for food again at 9 o'clock at night. Neighbor said that Danny was home alone when Robbie came home from school and that his mother has not come back.

FEB. 14 Social worker talks to Mrs. Lloyd. He finds out Mrs. Lloyd has not had steady work for the past few months. Social worker notices scars on Robbie's legs. Robbie said his mother beat him with a strap. Mrs. Lloyd said she does beat him when he misbehaves.

FEB. 15   Social worker reports possible case of child abuse and neglect to juvenile court. Social worker writes up a petition which states the reasons why the case of Robbie and Danny Lloyd is being brought to court.

In The Circuit Court Of Jackson County, Missouri
Juvenile Division
Kansas City, Missouri 64108
625 E. 26th Street

P E T I T I O N

IN THE INTEREST OF:

Robert Lloyd/Daniel Lloyd   PETITION NO. __64807__ .
NAME

__1042 Woodacre__   FILE NO. __39288__ .
ADDRESS

__4-21-72/1-31-77__
BIRTHDATE

The parents or legal guardian of the child/children are:

father deceased   /   Mary Lloyd

            (Father)   **(Mother)**

and they reside at:

1042 Woodacre

The person having legal custody of the child/children is:

Mother

Comes now the Juvenile Officer, within and for Jackson County, Missouri, and alleges that the child is within Jackson County, Missouri, and is in need of the care, treatment and services of the court because:

The environment of Robbie Lloyd and Danny Lloyd is harmful to their own welfare because the person legally responsible for their proper care and supervision fails, or is unable, to properly provide such, in that:

Robbie and Danny are left alone at home continually for several hours at a time

there is unsafe heating in their apartment

Robbie shows scars resulting from being whipped with a strap

Mrs. Lloyd does not feed the boys properly

Mrs. Lloyd has not been able to hold a steady job

Petitioner states that this is a physically, psychologically, and emotionally harmful environment for the children to live in.

WHEREFORE, petitioner prays the court to sustain this petition and to order appropriate supervision, care, examination, treatment, detention, placement, commitment, change of custody, or other disposition of said child as provided under provisions of chapter 211, R.S.Mo as amended.

A copy of the foregoing petition mailed/delivered this __15th__ day of __Feb.__ 19__79__ to __Legal Aid__, Attorney for said child.

Barry Horwitz
Juvenile Officer of Jackson County, Missouri

By _____

_____   _____
JUVENILE OFFICER   **DEPUTY**

61

FEB. 16   Social worker takes Robbie and Danny Loyd and places them in foster care until the hearing.

FEB. 19   Mrs. Lloyd receives notice from juvenile court that she must appear for a court hearing.

In The Circuit Court Of Jackson County, Missouri Juvenile Division

Kansas City, Missouri 64108

625 E. 26th Street

NOTICE TO PARENT/GUARDIAN, CHILD OF COURT HEARING

Robert & Daniel Lloyd	PETITION NO. 64807
IN THE INTEREST OF	**FILE NO. 39288**
1042 Woodacre	
ADDRESS	
4-21-72/1-31-77	
BIRTHDATE	

Enclosed is a copy of the Petition/Motion to Modify filed in the interest of the above named child(ren). If you have obtained an attorney to represent your child(ren), I would appreciate being notified as to his name. Thank you for your co-operation in this matter.

The Court Hearing is set for:

DAY:
DATE:
TIME:

Sincerely,

Administrative Supervisor

FORM 044-COR
3-5M-7/76

Note to students: Fill in the DAY, DATE, and TIME of the hearing with the day, date, and time when your class plans to hold this hearing.

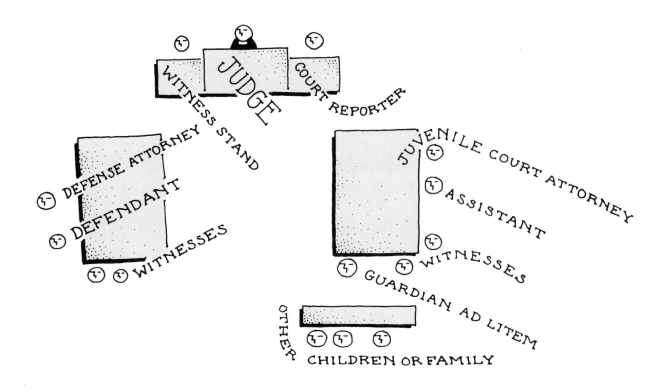

For your hearing you will need people to take the roles of:

Judge
Court reporter
Clerk
Bailiff
Juvenile court attorney/attorney's
    assistant
Defense attorney/attorney's
    assistant

Guardian ad litem
Mrs. Mary Lloyd, mother
Robbie Lloyd, juvenile
Mrs. Martha Cooper, grandmother
Mr. Barry Horwitz, social worker

TO PREPARE FOR THE HEARING

Read through the following descriptions for the hearing. After reading what is expected of each person, decide who will play each role at your hearing.

1. **Juvenile Court Attorney**—one student can be the attorney and one can be the attorney's assistant.

The juvenile court attorney's job is to prove with "clear and convincing evidence" that Robbie's and Danny's situation is harmful to them. You must prove that, for the reasons stated in the petition, the environment Robbie and Danny live in is harmful to their welfare. Your job is not to prove that their mother is guilty of any crime but to prove that the children are in fact being abused and neglected.

To prepare for the hearing talk with the social worker and Robbie. Make sure you understand what their stories are. Think about the questions you plan to ask them during the hearing. Ask the judge to explain the types of questions you are not allowed to ask (page 67).

At the hearing you will call the social worker to the witness stand first. Then you will call Robbie to the stand.

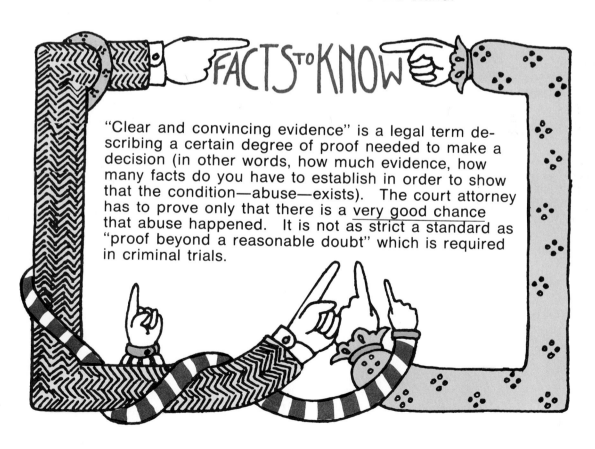

FACTS TO KNOW

"Clear and convincing evidence" is a legal term describing a certain degree of proof needed to make a decision (in other words, how much evidence, how many facts do you have to establish in order to show that the condition—abuse—exists). The court attorney has to prove only that there is a very good chance that abuse happened. It is not as strict a standard as "proof beyond a reasonable doubt" which is required in criminal trials.

2. **Defense Attorney** (for Mrs. Lloyd)—one student can be the defense attorney and one student can be the attorney's assistant.

Your job is to prove that Mrs. Lloyd is taking good enough care of her children, and that the juvenile court has no right to step in and tell Mrs. Lloyd what to do with her children.

At the hearing you should try to bring out information that is favorable to Mrs. Lloyd such as:

a. Mrs. Lloyd did not leave her boys alone except a few times when their grandmother didn't show up.

b. Mrs. Lloyd has little money, she heats the apartment, feeds and cares for her children the best she can with the little money she has.

c. Mrs. Lloyd cares about her children and wants them to live with her.

To prepare for the hearing talk to Mrs. Lloyd. Make sure you understand the story she will tell at the hearing. Think about the questions you will ask her and the other witnesses.

Ask the judge to explain the types of questions you are not allowed to ask (page 67).

Instructions to

It is your job to present the facts as YOU SEE THEM.

ROBBIE

You are the seven-year-old son of Mrs. Lloyd. This is your testimony. "I am seven years old. My brother, Danny, is two years old. I babysit him when my mom goes out. Sometimes she is gone when I get home from school and doesn't come home until after I go to bed. One day I stayed home from school to take care of Danny. I can do things for myself. I make my own breakfast every day. We don't have much food and I get hungry a lot. My favorite foods are potato chips and candy bars."

MRS. MARY LLOYD

You are the mother of two children. You are accused of abusing and neglecting your children. This is your testimony. "I am thirty-five years old. I work odd hours doing cleaning mostly. The boys' grandmother says she will babysit when I need to go out, then she doesn't show up. What am I supposed to do? We are poor. I do the best I can. I think Robbie is old enough to make his own breakfast and to look after Danny sometimes. I beat Robbie when he misbehaves. I think that is the best way to make him mind."

MRS. MARTHA COOPER, GRANDMOTHER

You are Mrs. Lloyd's mother and the grandmother of Robbie and Danny. This is your testimony. "I can babysit but I never know for sure when I'm supposed to. I can babysit at night but not during the day because of my job. My daughter doesn't like me messing in her business so I don't offer advice unless she asks me. There were a few times I didn't show up for babysitting because I got sick."

SOCIAL WORKER, MR. BARRY HORWITZ

You work for the Division of Family Services. You have been a social worker for 3 years. You investigate reports of child abuse. During the hearing the juvenile court attorney will ask you to give a full report on the case of Robbie and Danny Lloyd. This is your testimony:

"On Jan. 10 I called on the Lloyds to investigate the report made by their neighbor. I found that they lived in a small apartment. Only space heaters were used to heat the apartment. These are dangerous around young children. There was hardly any food and no phone in the home. Mrs. Lloyd said she only left her boys alone at home when it was necessary. She tried to get their grandmother to babysit, but she had no money to pay babysitters. On the first visit I warned her that it was dangerous to leave a seven year old alone with a two year old because in case of an emergency a seven year old would not know what to do. After the second Hot Line report I called on Mrs. Lloyd again. I found nothing changed in the apartment. I noticed scars on Robbie's legs that looked like they were made with a strap or an extension cord. Mrs. Lloyd admitted she beat Robbie with a strap to punish him. Mrs. Lloyd told me to mind my own business and leave her alone."

At this time reread the Report, read pages 59–61, and read over your testimony at the hearing, page 70. Based upon information contained in these readings decide what recommendation you will make to the judge concerning what should be done in this case. Write down your recommendation: include the reasons why you decided as you did. Before the hearing give a copy of your recommendation to the judge. Be prepared to explain your recommendation at the dispositional hearing.

In cases of child abuse and neglect a court can:

—order counseling for one or more family members
—order classes in parenting and child care
—allow a child to stay with the family under supervision of a social worker
—place a child in a foster home for a short time
—place a child in a foster home for a long time
—commit child or family member to be evaluated by doctors
—terminate (end completely) parental rights and have child adopted by another family

JUDGE

Your job is to listen to all the testimony. You sustain or overrule any objections made by the lawyers. Lawyers may not ask questions that:

1. Browbeat the witness
2. Are leading questions, such as, "You do think this boy is abused, don't you?"
3. Are biased questions, such as, "How can a mother like you be responsible for a child?"

(Before the hearing, explain to the lawyers that they are not allowed to ask these kinds of questions.)

After the lawyers have asked the witnesses questions, you may also question the witnesses or the lawyers if you don't understand something. It is your responsibility to decide if Robbie and Danny are being abused and neglected. Make your decision based on facts that are brought out at the hearing.

If you decide Robbie and Danny are abused and neglected, you must then decide what needs to be done about it. You will make this decision after you read and listen to the recommendation made by the social worker. The possible choices are on page 66.

THE COURT REPORTER

It is your job to take down every word that is said by the lawyers, judge, and witnesses during the hearing. In actual hearings court reporters have machines they use to take down every word quickly. The words you take down become a transcript. If, later on, someone had a question about the case, they would look at the transcript. Since you won't be able to use this machine, try to locate a tape-recorder that you could use the day of the hearing.

THE BAILIFF

Your job is to keep order in the courtroom. You take care of misconduct or an emergency; for example, if there is any unruly behavior or if someone faints or gets sick.

THE CLERK

Your job is to swear in the witnesses when they come up to the witness stand. It is also your job to handle any evidence or documents.

THE GUARDIAN AD LITEM

You are the lawyer who represents only the child. During the dispositional hearing when the court decides what should be done with the child, it is your job to make sure that the action taken is in the best interest of the child. You can ask the lawyers or any witness questions during the disposition part of the hearing.

A MOCK JUVENILE HEARING

I. THE ADJUDICATION

Bailiff: Please remain seated. The court of Judge _____ will come to order.

Judge: What do we have on the docket today?

Juvenile court attorney: This is the matter of Robert and Daniel Lloyd. The people present in the courtroom are (name all people present in courtroom who are involved in the case.)

The children, Robert, age 7, and Daniel, age 2, are in the courtroom. Shall I read the charges made in the petition?

Defense attorney: Yes.

Juvenile court attorney: (Reads the petition. Then says) Do you admit or deny this petition?

Defense attorney: I deny the petition.

Juvenile court attorney: I call _____ to the stand.
(name of first witness)

Judge: Be sworn in by the clerk.

Clerk: Hold up your right hand. Do you swear that the testimony you give in this cause will be the whole truth and nothing but the truth?

The juvenile court attorney begins questioning his or her witnesses. Then the defense attorney can cross-examine these witnesses. After all the witnesses for the juvenile court attorney have testified, the defense attorney may call witnesses. Each witness must be sworn in by the clerk before taking the stand.

FACTS TO KNOW

admit—means agree with, accept as true
deny—means disagree with, declare untrue
If the defense lawyer admits the petition, there is no need to prove the facts of the case. The disposition would start then.

Judge: (After hearing the testimony given by the witnesses and asking them questions of your own, you must decide if Robbie and Danny have suffered child abuse and neglect. State your decision to the court.)

If the judge decides that this is a case of child abuse, the hearing will move directly into the second part—the DISPOSITION. If the judge decides that there is no child abuse the hearing is over.

II. THE DISPOSITION (usually same time)

Juvenile court attorney: I want to call the social worker back to the stand. Have you made a careful study of the case of Robbie and Danny Lloyd? Are you ready to make a recommendation to the court?

Social worker: Yes, I have studied the case carefully. In the past month I was able to help Mrs. Lloyd find a steady job as a waitress. She will work in the evenings when her mother can babysit with the boys. The grandmother has agreed to do this. Mrs. Lloyd will have more money now to care for her family. I am still concerned that her way of punishing her boys could be harmful to them. Also of concern is the fact that Mrs. Lloyd does not know the value of good eating habits. She may not use her money to buy nutritious food for the boys, but rather may buy snack foods. She needs to purchase a better, safer heater for the apartment. She says she wants the boys with her. I am recommending _____ (at this point explain your recommendations to the court).

Guardian ad litem: (Questions the social worker to make sure that the recommendations are in the best interest of the boys.)

At this point, each of the lawyers and the judge may ask questions of anyone involved in the hearing. The mother, the grandmother, and Robbie can be questioned to make sure they are willing to follow through on their responsibilities.

Judge: (At the end of the discussion, the judge states the disposition.)

"It is therefore ordered that the juvenile be _____

_____

_____

_____

_____

1. Do you think the hearing was a fair way to resolve (work out) this problem of possible child abuse and neglect? Did you feel the judge's decision was fair to the children and to the parent? Explain your reasons.

2. Were all the facts necessary to decide the case brought out at the hearing?

3. If you had been the neighbor would you have called the child abuse Hot Line Service? Explain why or why not.

4. Social worker, explain the reasons you had for making the recommendation that you did. Explain any difficulties you had.

5. What if you were the judge in this case—what do you think about the way Mrs. Lloyd handled her boys? For example, do you think it was all right for her to leave Robbie and Danny at home alone?

6. What kind of help do you think it is most important for the Lloyd family to get?

7. What do you think needs to be done to help prevent child abuse and neglect?

8. What were some important things you learned from putting on your own mock juvenile hearing?

THEORY AND PRACTICE

JUVENILE COURT JUDGES

Objective: Students will be able to recognize the difference between theory and practice in certain aspects of the juvenile court.

Students will recognize that juvenile court judges are influenced by many facts when making decisions.

Students will recognize that a juvenile court judge has a responsibility to the individual juvenile as well as to society.

There are often gaps between the way things are supposed to be and the way things are. As with many things, in juvenile court some things are often different in THEORY (how it is supposed to be) than PRACTICE (how it actually is).

If, in practice, the juvenile courts fall short of the ideal, what should be done? Does that mean the whole idea should be tossed aside? Read on and continue to think about this question.

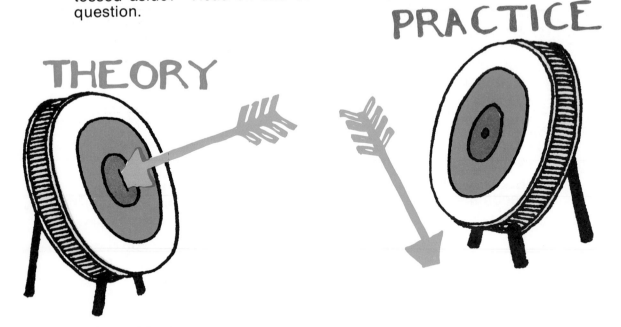

THEORY

PRACTICE

THEORY SAYS:

- The judge acts somewhat like a parent.
- He/she makes a careful study of the facts and decides what treatment will best help the juvenile and also protect society.
- Juvenile judges should have expert knowledge of law and child psychology.
- They should know about effective treatment programs for youth and be able to send young people to the program that will help them most.

PRACTICE SHOWS:

- Many judges treat juveniles the same as adult offenders.
- Many don't have adequate experience in juvenile court philosophy and procedure.
- Many have no special training in child psychology.
- Because of heavy case loads and limited number of juvenile courts, judges haven't time to research the available treatment programs carefully. In addition, effective training programs or group homes may be overcrowded or unavailable.

The next activity might help you understand more about how juvenile judges decide a case.

Judges have different opinions about things just as other people do. Judges must make very important decisions about what to do with juveniles. These decisions are often difficult because the judge has to consider what is best for the juvenile as well as what is best for the society. Different judges have different opinions about what to do with juveniles.

All people have different likes and dislikes, different opinions about things and different reasons for those opinions. See what your opinion is about food for a new restaurant.

PRETEND YOU ARE OPENING A NEW RESTAURANT

_____'s NEW RESTAURANT
OPENING SOON!

(Put your name on the line)

You are opening a new restaurant. Choose one kind of food that is your favorite.

Now, present the reasons you have for choosing to serve only this kind of food in your restaurant.

Can you explain why people have different opinions about foods?

Although this would not happen, let's pretend that there are three juvenile judges who must make a decision on one juvenile's case. The juvenile is Frank Jones who was found to have committed a purse snatching in Lesson 11. Now three judges must decide what to do with Frank.

They have to choose **one** of the four alternatives listed here:

1. Let Frank go with a warning.

2. Put Frank on probation in the care of his mother for six months. He would have to report to his juvenile officer once a week.

3. Send Frank to a group home.

4. Send Frank to a state institution for boys.

76

Judge Victoria Hasco—

My name is Judge Victoria Hasco. I have five children and I believe in punishing them if they misbehave. I do like children very much and believe they should be treated fairly. Some people say I should be a stricter judge and others say that I am too strict. I want to protect both the rights of the individual young person and the rights of society to be protected from crime. It is a difficult job.

What will I do with Frank?

Judge Samuel Ackman—

My name is Judge Samuel Ackman. I just came to the juvenile court from the family and divorce courts. The city and the state do not have adequate centers to treat juveniles so that delinquent juveniles can get help. Because there are no places to send juveniles, I try to put them back in their homes and give them adequate care with a counselor.

What will I do with Frank?

Judge James Taft—

My name is Judge James Taft. I have been a judge for 12 years. I live in the city with my wife and two sons. In the last four years, juvenile crime in my city has doubled and the city is blaming me. I won't stand for any more juveniles committing crimes. If I punish Frank severely perhaps it will influence other juveniles not to commit crimes. My wife had her purse stolen last year. I am responsible for protecting society.

What will I do with Frank?

QUESTIONS FOR DISCUSSION:

1. Did each judge decide to handle the case of Frank Jones differently? Why do you think there were these differences?

2. If Frank were sent to a state institution for boys, what do you think he would be like when he came out? Would he ever steal a purse again? Would he commit other offenses? What reasons do you have for your answer?

3. When Judge Victoria Hasco said that she "wanted to protect both the rights of society and the rights of the individual" what did she mean?

4. Judges are often limited in their decisions about what to do with juveniles because the available alternatives aren't as effective as they could be. Discuss the following "what if" situations.

 you as judge knew the probation officer had many more cases than he or she could effectively handle?

 you knew the state institution was overcrowded?

 you knew the group home that accepted Frank also had some juveniles who had committed very serious crimes?

 Frank's mother was unable to take care of him or supervise him very well?

Do these "what if" problems make a difference in your decision about what to do with Frank?

78

EXTRA!

You might want to keep a personal journal of your opinions concerning *Juvenile Problems and Law.* Lessons in this book often ask your opinion and the reasons for those opinions. You might keep all of your thoughts together in this journal and when you finish this book see if any of your opinions have changed.

PERSONAL	JOURNAL	
ON		
JUVENILE	PROBLEMS	
AND	LAW	
NAME:		
DATE:		
QUESTIONS	MY OPINIONS	MY REASONS

THEORY AND PRACTICE STATUS OFFENDERS

Objective: Students will be able to explain what it means to be a status offender.

Students will be able to discuss alternative ways to treat status offenders.

A status offense is an act which is illegal only if committed by a young person. For example, it is illegal for a 14-year-old to run away from home but it is not illegal for a 24-year-old to run away from home.

Some status offenses are running away from home, and being truant from school. What are some other status offenses?

There is a gap between theory and practice in handling status offenders.

THEORY SAYS:

The juvenile court has a right to take control of a juvenile if he or she is in need of supervision, but has not committed a "crime".

PRACTICE SHOWS:

Juveniles who are status offenders enter the juvenile court system and can be placed with young people who have committed more serious crimes. Status offenders can begin to see themselves as law-breakers rather than as people needing help.

be a juvenile court judge.

Pretend you are the juvenile judge who has to decide the following cases. You can choose the decision you think is best from the list following each case. You must give reasons to support the decisions you make.

James

James is 13. He has not attended school regularly for six months. By law James is required to attend school until he is 16. According to the juvenile code of his state, James was found to be truant from school and was taken into custody by the juvenile court. James' parents both work. They say they don't really care if James goes to school or not. They are too busy every day to make sure James goes to and stays at school. James says school is worthless. He likes spending time with older friends who don't go to school either.

Every judge has a responsibility to protect the community. This responsibility must be weighed against the desire to help a young person.

POINTS TO DISCUSS BEFORE MAKING DECISION: Is it harmful to society when James remains truant from school? In what ways might it hurt society if young people don't go to school? In what ways might it hurt James to be truant from school? As judge you could:

1) Not accept James in the juvenile court system and recommend that he go to a help center in the area.

2) Place him on probation with the requirement he must go to school and report to his juvenile officer once a week. His probation can last from two months to one year.

3) Send him away from home for one year to a training school.

4) Place him in a state institution for boys for six months.

5) Make the parents pay a fine if James does not go to school.

6) Your own idea: _____

_____

What is your decision? Give a good reason why you decided the way you did.

Carla

Carla was taken into custody by the juvenile court for being a runaway. This is the second time she has come to juvenile court for running away. The first time was one year ago. At that time she was placed on probation and had to report to a juvenile officer once a week for six months. Carla is 15 years old. She has no father and Carla's mother says she can't control Carla anymore. Carla says she is unhappy and bored at home. She has stayed with other runaways in "crash" houses and apartments. She has not gotten into any serious trouble during her runaway trips. She stays away from home about three weeks and then returns.

Discuss: In what way might young runaways hurt society? In what ways might young runaways be hurting themselves?

As judge you could:

1. Let Carla go and recommend that she go to a neighborhood help center.
2. Place Carla on probation with the requirement she must stay at home and report to a juvenile officer once a week.
3. Send Carla away to a training program for a few months.
4. Place Carla in a state institution for girls for six months.
5. Your own idea: _____

_____

What is your decision? Give a good reason for deciding the way you did.

Young people come into court as status offenders because they have problems. Their problems often affect the community. The juvenile court seems to be the best agency to take custody of these young people. Greater efforts could be made to keep these juveniles separate from those who have committed crimes.

Young people who are status offenders should never come to juvenile court. They are not really criminals but people in need of help. There should be other places these young people can get help.

Who do you think should take responsibility for young people, like James and Carla, who are status offenders?

Choose your answer from the list below:

—their parents or families

—other young people who have had counseling training

—the juvenile court system which includes places like training schools and foster homes

—other help centers run by churches or social service agencies with adult counselors and doctors

—no one. Let the young people take care of themselves

—specially trained people at public schools

—your ideas _____

JURY TRIALS FOR JUVENILES

Objective: Students will be able to discuss the pros and cons of having jury trials for juveniles.

A  facing the juvenile courts today is: Should juveniles be given the right to trial by jury?

A recent case, *McKeiver vs. Pennsylvania* (91 S.Ct. 1976) brought this question before the United States Supreme Court.

McKeiver vs *Pennsylvania:*

In Pennsylvania, John McKeiver was accused of robbery, larceny, and receiving stolen goods as acts of juvenile delinquency. At the hearing his parents requested he have a trial by jury. This request was denied. The judge decided that John McKeiver had violated the law. His case was then appealed (taken to a higher court) on the ground that because a jury trial had been denied he did not get a fair trial.

Organize a debate. To help you think about this question, read the reasons some people give for supporting jury trials for juveniles. Then read some reasons people give for being against them.

Reasons in favor of jury trials:

1. The Sixth Amendment to the Constitution states that "In all criminal prosecutions the accused shall have the right to a speedy and public trial by an impartial JURY. . . ." A juvenile should be given this right the same as an adult.

2. The U.S. Constitution requires that people be given "due process" or fair treatment under law when they are on trial. Trial by jury is necessary to make sure young people are given fair treatment.

3. Even though juvenile rehabilitation programs exist, for many young people these are the same as being "locked up." Juveniles have the right to a jury trial before their freedom is taken away.

Reasons against jury trials:

1. The purpose of a juvenile hearing is to do what is in the best interests of the juvenile. Jury trials would make the proceeding just like adult criminal trials. No one would care about helping the juvenile. The lawyers would only care about winning a case.

2. It is important that juvenile offenders be brought to court as quickly as possible. Jury trials would drag out the time a juvenile is involved with the courts.

3. There is no reason to believe that having a jury trial really makes a trial any more fair. Juries could be prejudiced and make bad decisions, too.

Which side of this question are you on?

Divide the class into six debate teams. Three teams will be **for** jury trials for juveniles and three will be **against** having jury trials. Each team should work together in preparing their arguments. Each team member could speak on a different part of the debate question.

In preparing your arguments for the debate, think about these questions:

1. Would you say that not having a jury trial makes a juvenile feel he/she is being treated unfairly? What effect might these feelings have on the juvenile?

2. If it was decided to have jury trials for juveniles, how old should the members of the jury be?

3. The juvenile court system is not perfect, but would having jury trials for juveniles improve the situation or worsen it?

RULES FOR THE DEBATE

1. A judge or panel of judges should decide which team wins the debate. The judge or judges keep score of how well each team argues its side of the debate according to debate rules.

2. A debater "For" the question begins with an argument in favor of having jury trials for juveniles. If the argument is reasonable the judges give that team one point.

3. Then, a debater "Against" the question must speak directly against the argument that was just made. It is difficult not to bring up new information, but it is necessary to speak against the argument made by the other team. If the debater does this and it sounds reasonable the judges give that team one point.

4. Now, a debater on the "Against" side gets to raise a new argument. If it is reasonable, that member's team gets a point. Then, it is the turn of the other team to speak directly against the argument just made. This procedure continues until all the arguments have been raised and responded to.

5. No person on one team can do all the debating.

ON TO THE DEBATE !

There are many people—parents, people who work with juveniles, and young people like you—who want to know more about how the juvenile justice system works. They need factual information concerning the juvenile court. Your class could sponsor a program for the school parents' association meeting to provide some information on the juvenile court.

As your speaker, you could invite a judge of the juvenile court in your community or a court social worker or counselor. The class could submit to the speaker a list of several questions which you, as a group, decide are the most urgent. This list should be sent at least a week before the date of the meeting. Such a list would help the speaker know exactly which aspects of the court's work your group most wants to know about.

You will have to work closely with the program chairperson or president of the parents' organization which is sponsoring the meeting. You may want to help distribute their meeting announcements. Plan carefully for the program. The speaker should know how much time he/she has on the program. He/she should also be asked to plan on ten or fifteen minutes for questions from the audience.

Of course the entire class should attend the meeting. Perhaps the parents' group would like some members of the class to act as hosts and hostesses for the meeting. By getting involved, you will learn more about the juvenile court. You will also show the school staff and your parents that you are interested and concerned.

Objective: **Students will be able to define a list of words introduced in Section II.**

You've already seen these words in the previous lessons. Do you know the meaning of each of them now? Write the definition for as many words as you can. Ask a classmate to check your work. Check your definition with the one in the glossary to see if it's correct. Write the correct definition for any word you missed.

hearing _____

juvenile court _____

delinquent _____

status offense_____

adjudicatory hearing _____

detention _____

dispositional hearing _____

take into custody _____

Make up at least 5 sentences that leave the last word to be filled in by a classmate. An example might be: An adult who is accused of a crime has a trial, but a juvenile has a

_____ .

NEWSBULLETIN REVIEW—SECTION II

Objective: Students will be able to answer questions on a class test about information presented in Section II.

Note to students: This lesson is a review quiz. You can use it to check how much you have learned so far about juvenile legal problems. Some classes have turned these reviews into newsbulletins. When your answers get printed in a newsbulletin, they help other people learn what you have learned.

Editorial

Write an editorial which takes a stand, FOR or AGAINST, on juveniles being treated like adults in court.

True/False

1. To go to juvenile court you must have broken a law.

   _____

2. A status offender is a young person who commits very serious crimes.

   _____

3. Juvenile counselors study the background of each juvenile who comes to court.

   _____

4. To be found delinquent means to be found guilty in juvenile court.

   _____

Drinking Law

In some states young people under 21 cannot be served alcoholic beverages.

Explain why you agree or disagree with this law.

Juvenile Court/Adult Court

What are two differences between how the juvenile court handles people and how the adult criminal court handles people?

1.

2.

Cartoon

Draw a picture showing a law just for young people.

The next section deals with juvenile crime—What should be done?

The following pages will provide you with some

SECTION III JUVENILE CRIME —WHAT SHOULD BE DONE? CRIME AND CONSEQUENCES

Objective: Students will be able to explain why certain acts are considered crimes by law.

Students will be able to recognize possible consequences of crime to the person who commits the crime.

What are the people doing in these pictures? Who is being harmed? What harm, if any, is being done?

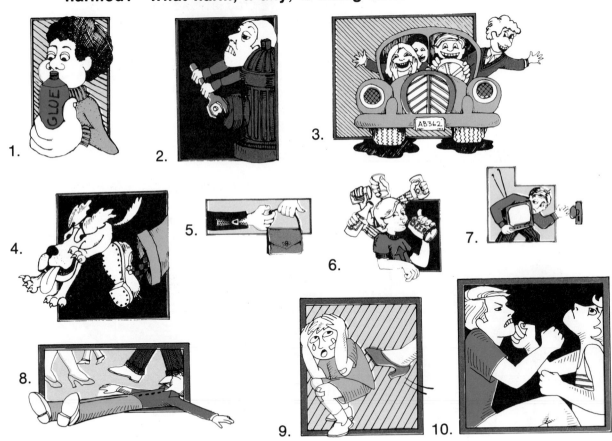

Look at the pictures on the preceding page. A crime is an act that is forbidden by law or the failure to do an act that the law requires.

1. Which of the actions pictured do you think should be considered a crime? Give reasons to back up your answers.

2. Rank these pictures (1–10) by placing the action that you think is the most serious first, the next most serious, second, and so on.

    Compare your rank-ordered lists in class and discuss the reasons people gave for ranking these actions the way they did.

The law says certain acts that harm society are crimes.
The law then separates crimes into three categories:

- Petty offenses—less serious, such as traffic violations, littering.

- Misdemeanors—more serious crimes such as drinking while driving, simple assaults, shoplifting.

- Felonies—very serious crimes such as robbery, murder, rape, assault with a deadly weapon.

3. Which of the actions pictured do you think should be petty offenses? Which ones do you think should be misdemeanors? Which ones do you think should be felonies?

Look at the pictures on page 92 again. Do you think the person (or persons) committing each act thought about its consequences? (A consequence is what happens as the result of an action taken.) For example:

A consequence of

might be

The following situations describe actions taken by juveniles. What might possible consequences of these actions be? Divide the class into pairs. The task of each pair is to write a newspaper headline and a story to go with it for each of the five situations given. The story should explain the consequences of what the people did in these situations.

Two boys were walking late at night. One boy said to the other, "This parking lot is closed at night. Let's climb over the fence and see what's inside." Possible headline: YOUNG BOY CLIMBING FENCE IS MAULED BY DOG

POSSIBLE STORY: Two thirteen-year-old boys climbed over a fence at Jackson's Used Cars, 4130 Grace. One of the boys was badly hurt when a watch dog attacked him. The other boy said that they did not see the dog approaching. "The dog seemed to come out of nowhere," he said. The hospitalized boy is in serious condition.

1. A group of young people were drinking beer at George's house. They decided to take George's mother's car. "My mother won't care," said George. "Nothing will happen."

   Possible headline: _____

   Possible story:

2. "I'm running away," thought Janet. "I'll hitchhike to my friend's place in California."

   Possible headline: _____

   Possible story:

3. "I'll look out for you," eighteen-year-old Brad told thirteen-year-old Allen. "You're still a juvenile. Just hold the knife on the old man while I take his wallet."

   Possible headline: _____

   Possible story:

4. "This glue smells terrific. Sniffing glue can't hurt me."

   Possible headline: _____

   Possible story:

5. "The old lady will let go of her purse when you grab it, don't worry," Ed said to Manuel.

   Possible headline: _____

   Possible story:

THINK about your five headlines and stories. Could they really happen? Then as a class listen while each group reads its headlines and stories. Discuss them. Which ones did you think were most realistic? Least realistic? Explain why.

Consequences to Other People

Objective: **Students will recognize short and long range consequences of crime for the victim.**

Crime brings harmful consequences to the victims against whom it is committed. Often a crime indirectly affects more people than just the victim.

The following stories came from interviewing victims of crimes and victims' families. No pictures are included. As you read these statements make up a picture in your mind of the person who is talking and try to feel what that person is feeling.

I always wanted to be an airline pilot. I had just finished the written examination. A speeding car full of kids forced me off the road. Glass from the windshield cut my eyes. Now there is no way I can be an airline pilot.

On my way to the store, two teenage girls stole my purse. I have no money for my medicine. I have no money for my groceries. I am all alone. What am I to do?

My husband was attending a convention. Some kid hit him on the head with a ball bat. He never carried more than three or four dollars. There is brain damage. He may have to undergo surgery again. Our five children are young. What am I going to do?

How does crime affect people's lives?

Read several stories concerning crimes. Imagine how the victims' lives might be changed as a result of the crimes. Do you think the crimes changed the lives of the family members of the victims? Use your imagination. Think about how a victim's life style might be changed, perhaps for years, as a result of the crime. You might want to work in groups. Select newspaper stories. Then share with the rest of the class your ideas about what might happen to victims of crime.

Note to students: For more on what you can do to aid victims, see the Community Involvement Project on the next page.

98

What can you do to aid victims of crime?

One project would be to write to a local aid-to-victims group and find out how you can help. Perhaps they need you to collect canned goods, or clothing, or provide some specific service for the victim or victims' family.

The organization would probably welcome your help in making the community aware of the kind of help they offer to victims. You could write an article for the local neighborhood newspaper describing the group and what they do. Or you could write a letter to the newspaper explaining how important groups like this are to the community.

Consequences of Crime for the Community

Objective: Students will be able to recognize consequences of shoplifting and vandalism for the entire community.

We've discussed possible consequences for people who commit crimes and for the victims of crimes. Crime can also have major consequences for a community. In this lesson we will see how two kinds of crime, shoplifting and vandalism, can affect a community.

The consequences of shoplifting are more than just this.

One young person gave this example of what can happen as a result of shoplifting:

> "My father used to own a grocery store. People from all over the neighborhood shopped there. All the kids came in for candy, apples, potato chips—you name it. My dad said it wasn't just the shoplifting that made him close down, but that was the straw that broke the camel's back."

Do you know what his father meant?

Shoplifting forces stores to raise their prices to pay for their losses. Everyone who buys at the store must pay higher prices for goods in stores where there is frequent shoplifting. Sometimes stores close down or leave a neighborhood because people stop shopping there when prices go up or because the store loses so much money from having merchandise stolen.

What are some problems people in a neighborhood have when stores move away?

Did you know?

In just one year, businesses in this country lost four billion dollars through shoplifting, internal theft, and bookkeeping errors.

Stores which suffer from shoplifting must pay for burglar alarms, hidden cameras, security guards, and other security systems. The stores raise the prices of their goods in order to have these security systems and still stay in business.

In the end, who suffers most from shoplifting?

VANDALISM: The deliberate, malicious destruction of property

"My mother suggested a great family project. We'd all work on fixing up a four-family apartment building. The best apartment building for the money was just about ten blocks from our house. We had decided to buy it! We all went back to the building with the real estate agent to have one last look. When we arrived the police were there. They had caught three kids who had vandalized the building. They broke the windows and the water pipes. The water ruined the furnaces. Mom said the cost of fixing the building is just too much now. We can't afford the extra expense. I'm so mad. Why did they do such a dumb thing?"

How might this act of vandalism affect this neighborhood?

"Our superintendent of schools explained that the cost of replacing windows and repairing vandalized school property has risen to a new high. The new text books planned for the tenth grade cannot be bought. There just isn't enough money left in the budget. In fact the superintendent is not even certain that there will be enough money left to pay for the present athletic program. The cost of building materials has risen, and the incidents of vandalism to school buildings just keep increasing."

Has your school or school system suffered from vandalism? List different types of vandalism that you feel have hurt your school.

Does vandalism have any effect on how people feel about your school? Has vandalism affected any of your school programs?

Note to students: For more on what you can do to stop school vandalism, see the Community Involvement Project on the next page.

A community involvement project gives you and your classmates a chance to take what you have learned inside the classroom outside the classroom to help the community.

Your class could do a study of the cost of vandalism to your school or school system. Talk to your principal about the idea. With his/her permission write to the superintendent of your school system. Ask for information on vandalism to the schools during the last few years. The building department might have detailed figures showing the cost of repairing broken windows. How would broken windows affect heating costs? What about the cost of removing the writing on walls in the buildings? How many desks have to be replaced because of deliberate damage?

You might want to ask for a copy of the school system budget. (It is likely to be a thick book.) You could compare the cost of textbooks or athletic supplies to the cost of vandalism. What could the system buy for students if it did not have to spend so much on vandalism?

When your class completes its report, send a copy to the superintendent.

You also might hold a meeting to present the results of your study to the entire school or to the parent association. Invite police officers in the neighborhood and community people. Let the community know that you care about what is happening.

DISPOSITIONAL ALTERNATIVES

Objective: **Students will be able to describe four dispositional alternatives.**

Students will decide appropriate dispositional alternatives for certain cases.

This boy is stealing **A** bike. What do you think should happen to him?

THIS BOY is stealing a bike. What do you think should happen to him?

This boy is stealing **YOUR** bike. What do you think should happen to him?

YOUR FRIEND is stealing a bike. What do you think should happen to him?

1. What do you think should happen to the bike thief in each of the four situations?
2. What are the differences in these four situations?
3. Were these differences important to you in deciding what you think should happen to him? Explain your answer.

To decide what should happen to people who break the law is a responsibility of the legal system. In juvenile court the juvenile judge has the responsibility to decide what to do with young people who come before the court. The choices the judge has are called **Dispositional Alternatives**. Here are the ones most commonly used:

A Warning
Juveniles are not given a sentence but are warned that if they come to court again the court will take more severe action.

Probation Counseling
Juveniles stay in their own homes and continue their usual activities. A deputy juvenile officer or juvenile counselor sees them regularly. During these counseling periods it can be learned if they are fulfilling their responsibilities to school, work, and families.

Group Home
A large house, usually in the juvenile's own community. About ten or twelve young people live in the house with counselors who live and work there. Juveniles are free to come and go about their usual activities. The juveniles are responsible for going to school or work. The resident counselors check to make certain the juveniles are meeting these responsibilities. Each juvenile takes part in household activities, like cleaning, etc.

Restitution
The juveniles are ordered to pay back the victims in some way for the harm caused them.

Foster Care

Juveniles who have very serious problems at home can be placed in another home. Families agree to "take in" young people and make them part of their family. Counseling times with the juvenile take place regularly.

Minimum Security Center

Smaller place where juveniles are not locked in but where they must stay. Emphasis here is on educational activities and training programs. Juveniles are kept under close watch; most of their daily activities are set up for them.

Maximum Security Center

Large state institution housing about 500 boys or girls. Many states have one place for boys and one for girls, usually they are outside major city areas. Juveniles are kept under close watch and their daily activities are entirely set up for them. Young people are locked in and can not leave. Activities in these institutions change, but usually juveniles are required to attend some kind of school while they are there.

Certification As An Adult

Juveniles may be certified as adults under certain conditions. As adults their cases are tried in adult criminal court and they may receive an adult penalty. Juveniles can be certified as adults for serious crimes such as armed robbery, murder, rape, or if they have a long record of serious violations.

Use the dispositional alternatives on the previous pages in deciding what should happen to the juveniles in the following stories. Explain the decision you made in detail. If you decide to give a warning, what would you say? If you decide to place a juvenile in a home or institution, how long would he or she have to stay? If you decide to make the juvenile pay back the victim, in what way would payment be made?

In making your decision, remember that the responsibility a juvenile judge has is to help a young person change for the better and also to protect society from being harmed by juvenile lawbreakers. In each of these stories the judge found the juveniles delinquent. You must decide what disposition will be made in each case.

Story I

Jeff said to Danny, "Old man Daws didn't have any right to kick us out of his store and call us bums. Let's get his store tonight. We'll show him he can't get away with treating us like dirt." These boys were caught by the police throwing bricks into Mr. Daws' store window. The police took the boys (ages 14 and 15) to the juvenile court.

What dispositional alternative will you choose for Jeff and Danny? Explain your reasons.

Story II

Charlie and his friends didn't have anything to do one afternoon. They passed a house that no one lived in. "Let's tear the place up," said Juan. As they were messing up the house, two police officers came and took them into custody. Charlie told the police they were just having a good time. They weren't doing anything wrong since no one lived in the house anyway. The police officer said, "It doesn't matter that no one lives in this house. The house is private property and it is against the law to vandalize it."

What dispositional alternative will you choose for these juveniles? Explain your reasons.

Story III

Mack wanted some spending money. He tried to get a part-time job after school but couldn't find one. A friend said, "A quick way to make a lot of money is to break into houses and steal stereos and TVs. I know people who will take the stolen goods off your hands fast and pay you good money for them." Mack and his friend, George, decided to try it. They were picked up by the police their first night out.

What dispositional alternative will you choose for Mack and George? Explain your reasons.

Story IV

Susan really wanted the latest albums that all of her friends already had. She had no money. She had taken small things from stores before and had been to juvenile court, but was let go with a warning. She walked into Hifi Record Shop, took the records, and left. A salesman ran after her and stopped her on the street. He called the police. Susan was taken into custody for shoplifting and referred to the juvenile court.

What dispositional alternative will you choose for Susan? Explain your reasons.

Rehabilitation or Punishment

LESSON 22

Objective: Students will be able to explain the terms "rehabilitation" and "punishment".

Students will analyze different points of view concerning rehabilitation and punishment for juvenile offenders.

"Treat him like an adult."

"Provide a special kind of place to rehabilitate him."

"Just lock him up."

"Understand him, he's had many problems in his young life."

"According to our law the punishment for his crime has been set at . . . ."

People disagree about how a juvenile who has broken the law should be handled by the juvenile court.

These people are for stricter punishments for juveniles who commit crimes. What arguments might they be making for stricter punishments?

These people are for helping young people change to a way of life that is more acceptable to society. They want to make sure young people get help. What arguments might they be making for their position?

rehABILITATION

Rehabilitation emphasizes restoring a person to a way of life which is useful and acceptable to society.

Name some types of activities or programs a young person might take part in that might help in his/her rehabilitation.

Punishment emphasizes protection of society by taking offenders off the streets. It also emphasizes deterrence—making the consequences (being locked up in prison) bad enought to be an example to others not to commit crimes.

PUNISHMENT

Describe this picture. Do you think this a realistic way to describe punishment? Explain your answer. Review the Dispositional Alternatives on pages 104–105. Which of these alternatives would you consider to be efforts to rehabilitate the juvenile? Which ones would you consider to be punishments?

This questionnaire is intended to help people better understand what their opinions are about rehabilitation and punishment for juvenile offenders.

Circle the opinion closest to yours for each answer:

SA   Strongly agree
A   Agree
O   No opinion
D   Disagree
SD   Strongly disagree

1. "Taxpayers should spend money for better rehabilitation places (for juveniles) in our community."   SA   A   O   D   SD

2. "The only way to handle juvenile crime is to put kids in a place that will make them feel sorry for ever getting into trouble."   SA   A   O   D   SD

3. "The way to rehabilitate is to give kids an experience in a place where they know people care about them and where they have to meet certain responsibilities."   SA   A   O   D   SD

4. "If they spent more money making the schools better, they wouldn't need to spend the money on rehabilitation centers because fewer young people would get into trouble."   SA   A   O   D   SD

5. "Kids don't need to be re-habilitated, they just need to know they can't get away with committing crimes without being punished."   SA   A   O   D   SD

6. "If juveniles were given stiffer pun-ishment, there would not be as much juvenile crime."   SA   A   O   D   SD

7. "It depends on the person. All ju-venile offenders are different. Some should be worked with and helped, and some should just be locked up."   SA   A   O   D   SD

8. "To rehabilitate people to become useful members of society, you have to make certain they feel good about themselves, feel they have some worth as human beings."   SA   A   O   D   SD

9. "Juveniles who commit crimes should be given jail sentences not special 'help programs.'"   SA   A   O   D   SD

After answering these questions and discussing them as a class, you might want to take this questionnaire to two people you know and ask them to complete it. Then, bring back your findings and make a chart in class showing how people re-sponded to these questions.

SET PENALTIES FOR JUVENILES?

Objective: Students will be able to explain what it means to have set penalties for juvenile offenders.

Students will be able to give reasons in favor of and against having set penalties for juveniles.

In adult criminal courts there are set penalties for crimes. For example, some states have a set penalty of between one and five years for burglary. Penalties are set by federal, state, or local lawmakers. Some people want to change the law so that set penalties would also be given to juveniles who commit crimes. This means that juveniles would be given penalties according to the offense they committed, not according to their individual circumstances.

SHOULD THERE BE SET PENALTIES FOR JUVENILES BASED ON THE SERIOUSNESS OF THE OFFENSE RATHER THAN ON THE SPECIAL CIRCUMSTANCES OF EACH JUVENILE?

LIST **REASONS FOR** HAVING SET PENALTIES FOR JUVENILES

_____

_____

_____

_____

LIST **REASONS AGAINST** HAVING SET PENALTIES FOR JUVENILES

_____

_____

_____

_____

Apply the idea of giving set penalties for juvenile crimes in the following two cases.

THE CASE OF CARRIE WALLACE

Carrie is 15. Her boyfriend, Harry, is 17. Harry and his brother Steve decided they wanted a TV set. Carrie said she wanted to be in on whatever Harry did. The three of them planned how they would break into a house and steal a TV. Since Carrie was the smallest, she was chosen to slip into the basement window of the house and unlock the door for Harry and Steve. The police caught them with the TV set before they left the house. Carrie was taken into custody by the juvenile court. She was accused of burglary. At her hearing she was found delinquent. This is her first offense.

Do you think the judge should give Carrie a standard penalty set by law for burglary? Do you think the judge should give Carrie a penalty based upon any special circumstances of her case?

Give a well-thought out reason for your answer.

SLEEK'S CASE

"Sleek" was a member of the "Hornets," a tough teenage gang. He was 15 years old and had gained a reputation in the gang as a person not to mess around with. Frankie was Sleek's enemy. Frankie dated Sleek's girlfriend and Sleek vowed he would get him. Sleek jumped Frankie, pulled a knife and stabbed Frankie in the back. The police came, arrested Sleek and Frankie and sent Frankie to the hospital. Frankie recovered. Sleek had a previous record of aggravated assaults. His counselor knew Sleek lived in an area of the city where there were many teenage gangs. At his hearing Sleek was found delinquent.

Do you think the juvenile judge should give Sleek a standard penalty set by law for aggravated assault?

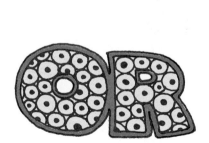

Do you think the judge should give Sleek a penalty based upon any special circumstances of his case?

Give a well-thought out reason for your answer.

Read All About It

You might be interested in learning more about changes in the way the juvenile courts in your state handle dispositional alternatives and punishments. Changes in these kinds of laws are made by state legislatures. You might write to your state legislator and request information about proposed changes or recent changes in juvenile court procedure in your state. Ask your state legislator to explain to you what he or she thinks of these laws. (Did he or she vote for them? Why? Why not?) In your letter explain that you are requesting this information because you are preparing a report as a school project. Perhaps two or three students could jointly write a letter. Think about and discuss which questions you most want the state legislator to answer. Don't forget to thank the state legislator for answering your questions.

Juveniles—Helping Themselves

Objective: Students will be able to discuss causes of juvenile offenses.

Students will be able to analyze ways to prevent juveniles from committing offenses.

People concerned with juvenile delinquency have many different views on how to stop juveniles from committing offenses and how to help them if they get into trouble with the law.

Young people get into trouble with the law because: _____

_____

_____

_____

_____

_____

Go back over your class list of reasons why young people break the law. For each cause you named, suggest some effective action that could be taken that might prevent this type of lawbreaker from breaking the law again.

118

Here is a list of illegal acts often committed by juveniles. Several reasons are given for each illegal act. Number the reasons (1, 2, etc.) in the order in which you think they reflect the thinking of young people who commit each act. If you think of a reason not already listed, write that reason in the space marked "other". In column two write a suggested way of preventing this type of illegal act.

Column 1

Offenses and possible reasons

Column 2

1. Juveniles shoplift because:

_____ they need what they take.

_____ it's a challenge not to get caught.

_____ they feel the store can afford the loss.

_____ they know they won't get a stiff penalty if they are caught.

_____ other _____

_____

Based on your first-ranked answer, what can be done to prevent shoplifting?

2. Juveniles use illegal drugs:

_____ to escape from their personal problems.

_____ to be cool.

_____ to do what their friends do.

_____ because they see their parents using alcohol and other drugs.

_____ other _____

_____

Based on your first-ranked answer, what can be done to prevent the illegal use of drugs?

3. Juveniles <u>destroy property</u> (<u>vandalize</u>):

—— because they are angry and don't know how else to show it.

—— to get back at someone.

—— for fun.

—— because they have never owned anything and don't know how it feels to have something you own wrecked.

—— other _____

_____

Based on your first-ranked answer, what can be done to prevent <u>vandalism</u>?

4. Juveniles commit <u>assault and battery</u> (see glossary):

—— to prove they are tough.

—— because they don't know how to talk out problems or anger.

—— picking on people makes them feel big.

—— they were beat up a lot when they were younger.

—— other _____

_____

Based on your first-ranked answer, what can be done to prevent <u>as-sault</u> or <u>assault and battery</u>?

As a class discuss the number one reason given for each of the four illegal acts. Did most people rank the same reason first? Were the suggested ways of preventing illegal acts realistic?

BECAUSE OF YOUR EXCELLENT WORK ON THE PREVIOUS
PAGES

the governor of _____ has just contacted you,
name of your state

_____, and has asked
your full name

to serve on the Governor's Commission on Juvenile Crime
Prevention.   You are to turn in a report working in a group of
five other selected commission members.   Your report should
include suggestions on how to deter (prevent) young people
from committing different kinds of offenses.   Describe in detail
how your suggestions would work.   Also, answer the following
questions and explain your answers in your report.

Should there be set penalties for juveniles?   Would that
reduce crime?

Should more money be spent for rehabilitation programs?
What kinds of programs do you think would be most
effective?

Should anyone over 14 found delinquent of a felony be
tried as an adult?

Should more money be put into prevention programs for
young people?   What kinds of programs?

Should there be a program for restitution in juvenile
courts?   How would it work?   What kinds of offenses
would be included?

Objective: Students will be able to define words introduced in Section III.

You have already seen these words in the previous lessons. Do you know the meaning of them right now? See if you can write the definition of each of these words. Check your definition with the one in the glossary to see if it is correct.

felony _____

victim _____

rehabilitation _____

misdemeanor _____

consequence _____

offense _____

Make up sentences using each of the above words correctly. Perhaps you can combine two or more words in one sentence. Your sentences must make sense.

NEWSBULLETIN REVIEW—SECTION III

Objective: Students will be able to answer questions on a test about information presented in Section III.

Note to students: This lesson is a review quiz. You can use it to check how much you have learned about juvenile problems and the juvenile justice system. Some classes have turned these reviews into newsbulletins. When your answers get printed in a newsbulletin, they help other people learn what you have learned.

Poster

Draw a poster urging people at your school to help with a problem involving juveniles and the law.

Editorial

What do you think would be the most effective action to take to prevent juvenile crime?

Complete the following sentences:

1. When people don't think about what might happen as a result of something they do, they don't think of the

   _____

2. An extremely serious crime is called a

   _____

3. A person against whom a crime is committed is called a

   _____

VANDALISM

SET PENALTIES FOR JUVENILES

Give one reason *for* having set penalties for juveniles.

_____

Give one reason *against* having set penalties for juveniles.

_____

Describe two ways vandalism hurts a neighborhood.

_____

_____

glossary

ADJUDICATORY HEARING	A hearing to decide whether or not a juvenile committed the offense of which he/she is accused. The facts of the case are brought out through questioning.
ALTERNATIVE	A choice between two or more possibilities.
ASSAULT	A threat and/or act carried out to use force on and harm another person.
CHILD ABUSE AND NEGLECT	A violation of the law in which the environment of a child is harmful to his/her welfare.
CONSEQUENCE	What happens as a result of an action taken.
COUNSEL (verb)	To give advice or guidance.
COUNSELOR	A person who helps others to solve their problems by giving advice or making suggestions.
CRIME	An act that is forbidden by law, or failure to do an act that the law requires.
DELINQUENT	Short for "juvenile delinquent"—a young person who has done an illegal act or seriously misbehaved.
DETENTION	Being kept in confinement or temporary custody.
DETENTION CENTER	The place where juveniles are held (in detention) while awaiting a hearing.
DETER	To prevent or discourage someone from acting.
DISPOSITION	A term used in juvenile court—similar to a sentence in adult court.
DISPOSITIONAL HEARING	A hearing to decide what should be done with a juvenile who has been found to be delinquent.

DUE PROCESS OF LAW	Fair treatment under the law, guaranteed by fourteenth amendment.
FELONY	A serious crime with a sentence of a year or more in prison.
FOURTEENTH AMENDMENT	Amendment to the United States Constitution which says that the states must give all citizens due process of law and equal protection of the laws.
GUARDIAN AD LITEM	A person (usually a lawyer) who is appointed by a court to take care of the interest of someone during a lawsuit or hearing.
JURISDICTION	Control over or authority within a specific geographic area, or over certain persons or issues.
JUVENILE	A young person, not yet adult. State laws establish the age for juveniles and the age at which the juvenile becomes an adult.
JUVENILE COURT	A court set up to handle cases of delinquent or neglected children.
JUVENILE HEARING	A court proceeding; a trial-like process that may take place in the juvenile judge's chambers or in a courtroom.
LEGAL PROCESS AND PROCEDURE	An action taken in court. The steps to be followed in making a court decision as established by law.
MINOR	A person under the age of full legal rights and duties.
MISDEMEANOR	A less serious offense than a felony. Usually punishable by a fine or less than a year in prison.
OFFENSE	A term used in juvenile law for a violation of the law.
PROBATION	A court sentence requiring a person to follow certain orders and undergo supervision.
PUNISHMENT	A penalty for wrongdoing. A penalty given a lawbreaker.

REHABILITATION	The restoration of a person to a way of life which is acceptable to society.
RESTITUTION	A type of sentence or disposition in which the lawbreaker is ordered to repay the victim for his/her loss or for harm done to him/her.
STATUS OFFENSE	Violation of a law which applies only to juveniles. An act which is made illegal if a juvenile commits it.
TAKE INTO CUSTODY	A term used in juvenile law—similar to arrest in an adult criminal proceeding.
TESTIMONY	The information a witness gives under oath in court.
VANDALISM	The deliberate, malicious destruction of property.
VICTIM	A person against whom a criminal act is committed.
WRIT OF HABEAS CORPUS	A procedure by which a person already in prison petitions to have the case reconsidered by a higher court. The writ directs the prison authorities who "have the body" of the prisoner to produce it for the hearing.

Appendix

Order of Disposition form

In The Circuit Court Of Jackson County, Missouri

IN THE INTEREST OF:

_____ PETITION NO: _____

MALE/FEMALE, BORN ____ FILE NO. _____

FINDING OF JURISDICTION AND ORDER OF DISPOSITION

Now on _____, there being present
_____, A Juvenile Officer of the Juvenile
Division of the Circuit Court of Jackson County, Missouri;

_____, A Social Service Worker of the Missouri
Division of Family Services; and

_____, Attorney for the Juvenile Officer;

_____, The Juvenile;

_____, His/Her Mother; and

_____, His/Her Father; and

_____, Attorney for the Juvenile;

And testimony being heard and other evidence received by the
Court, the Court finds that the allegations of the _____ Petition _____ Amended Petition are sustained, in that the:

_____ Allegations of the Petition are admitted

_____ Allegations of the Petition are admitted as amended

_____ Evidence adduced proves the allegations of the Petition

_____ Evidence adduced proves the allegations of the Petition as amended

_____ Count _____ dismissed with prejudice

_____ Count _____ dismissed without prejudice

And the Court has jurisdiction over the juvenile pursuant to the provisions of Section 211.031 R.S.Mo, and the Court having received further evidence concerning the need of said juvenile for care and treatment, and it being found that said juvenile is in need of care and treatment which can be furnished by _____

_____

IT IS THEREFORE ORDERED that said juvenile be ____

_____

_____

_____
JUDGE/COMMISSIONER

ACKNOWLEDGEMENTS

The people who helped us through the years in developing and refining the *Law in Action Series* are too numerous to give each of them the credit they deserve here. The teachers, administrators, students, parents, juvenile court personnel and law-related resource people each require a personal thank you.

We would like to say a special word of appreciation to Dr. Isidore Starr who has been a constant source of inspiration and guidance to us. Mary Curd has given excellent assistance in many facets of the revision. Trudy Faust has been invaluable as an editor and researcher. Susan Spiegel has provided legal help and guidance without which we could not have met our deadline. To Mary Engelbreit, who created many of the illustrations, thank you for your talent, skill, cooperation, and perceptiveness.

The responses of students to the material have been extremely valuable in revising *Juvenile Problems and the Law* for this Second Edition. Their overwhelming interest, frankness, and eagerness to learn about the law continues to make our endeavors worthwhile.

To our husbands, Richard Ackerly and Andrew Trivers and our parents, Dr. and Mrs. George Mahe and Mr. and Mrs. Max Riekes, who were always supporting us with encouraging helpful suggestions, very special thanks.

To everyone at West Publishing Company thanks for unfailing patience, understanding, and support.

Linda Riekes
Sally Mahe Ackerly